MANNERS AND RULES

OF

GOOD SOCIETY

OR SOLECISMS TO BE AVOIDED

BY A MEMBER
OF THE ARISTOCRACY

Elibron Classics
www.elibron.com

MANNERS AND RULES

OF

GOOD SOCIETY

MANNERS AND RULES

OF

GOOD SOCIETY

OR SOLECISMS TO BE AVOIDED

BY A MEMBER

OF THE ARISTOCRACY

THIRTY-THIRD EDITION

LONDON

FREDERICK WARNE AND CO.

AND NEW YORK

1911

PREFACE

"MANNERS AND RULES OF GOOD SOCIETY" contains all the information comprised in the original work, "Manners and Tone of Good Society," but with considerable additions. In a volume of this nature it is necessary to make constant revisions, and this is periodically done to keep it up to date, that it may be depended upon as being not only the most reliable, but also the *newest book of etiquette.*

A comparison of the number of chapters and their subjects with those of the early editions would best demonstrate how the work has grown, not merely in bulk, but in importance also. This extension has allowed many subjects to be more exhaustively treated than heretofore, and it now includes every rule and point that could possibly be comprehended in its title.

The work throughout its many editions has commended itself to the attention of thousands of readers, and it is hoped the present edition will be received by society in general with the marked success of its predecessors.

CONTENTS

viii CONTENTS

INTRODUCTORY REMARKS

THE title of this work sufficiently indicates the nature of its contents. The Usages of Good Society relate not only to good manners and to good breeding, but also to the proper etiquette to be observed on every occasion.

Not only are certain rules laid down, and minutely explained, but the most comprehensive instructions are given in each chapter respecting every form or phase of the subject under discussion that it may be clearly understood what *is* done, or what is *not* done, in good society, and also how what *is* done in good society should be done. It is precisely this knowledge that gives to men and women the consciousness of feeling thoroughly at ease in whatever sphere they may happen to move, and causes them to be considered well bred by all with whom they may come in contact.

A solecism may be perhaps in itself but a trifling matter, but in the eyes of society at large it assumes proportions of a magnified aspect, and reflects most disadvantageously upon the one by whom it is committed;

the direct inference being, that to be guilty of a solecism argues the offender to be unused to society, and consequently not on an equal footing with it. This society resents, and is not slow in making its disapproval felt by its demeanour towards the offender.

Tact and innate refinement, though of the greatest assistance to one unused to society, do not suffice of themselves; and although counting for much, cannot supply the want of the actual knowledge of what is customary in society. Where tact and innate refinement do not exist—and this is not seldom the case, as they are gifts bestowed upon the few rather than upon the many—then a thorough acquaintance with the social observances in force in society becomes more than ever necessary, and especially to those who, socially speaking, are desirous of making their way in the world.

Those individuals who have led secluded or isolated lives, or who have hitherto moved in other spheres than those wherein well-bred people move, will gather all the information necessary from these pages to render them thoroughly conversant with the manners and amenities of society.

This work will be found of equal service to both men and women, as in each chapter the points of social etiquette to be observed by both sexes have been fully considered.

Those having the charge of young ladies previous to their introduction into society, either mothers, chaperons, or governesses, will also derive much useful and practical information from the perusal of this work, while to those thoroughly versed in the usages of society it cannot fail to commend itself, containing as it does many useful and valuable hints on social questions.

MANNERS AND RULES OF
GOOD SOCIETY

CHAPTER I

THE MEANING OF ETIQUETTE

WHAT is etiquette, and what does the word convey? It is a poor one in itself, and falls very far short of its wide application. It has an old-fashioned ring about it, savouring of stiffness, primness, and punctiliousness, which renders it distasteful to many possessing advanced ideas; and yet the word etiquette is not so very old either, as Johnson did not include it in his dictionary, and Walker apologises for introducing it into his, and according to the authorities he quotes, it is supposed to be derived from stichos, stichus, stichetus, sticketta, and from thence to etiquette. But whether derived from the Latin or the French—and many incline to the latter opinion—there is no doubt that could a new word be found to replace this much abused one, it would be a welcome addition to our vocabulary. The word has unfortunately become associated in our minds with forms, ceremonies, and observances, in an exaggerated degree; and it has been so constantly misused and misinterpreted and misunderstood that ridicule and contempt have been most unjustly and unfairly thrown upon it. The true meaning of etiquette can hardly be described in dictionary parlance; it embraces the whole gamut of good manners, good breeding, and true politeness. One of the reasons which have no doubt contributed to bring the word "etiquette" into disrepute, is the manner in which the subject has been handled by incompetent people, who, having but a very hazy and obscure knowledge, if any knowledge at all, yet profess to write guides to polite manners—rambling and incoherent guides, which not only provoke a smile from those better informed, but mislead and bewilder any one rash enough to consult them, without previous inquiry as to whether they are safe to follow. A little caution on this head would insure the most correct and reliable work being secured amongst so much that is unreliable. Some people read everything that is written on the subject of etiquette, not only those who are ignorant and wish to learn something of its laws, but those who are thoroughly well versed in them and who, one might suppose, had nothing to learn; still these latter like to see what is written, to feel the satisfaction of being supported in their own knowledge by a well-informed writer; or of finding amusement in the absurdities gravely advanced by some one writing from another sphere than that where *savoir vivre* reigns. Others attach a very narrow meaning to the word etiquette, and neither accept it nor understand it in its true sense; they have an idea that its rules influence and govern society in general. Rules of etiquette are from their point of view but trammels and shackles; let them be cast off or burst through, say they; let every one do as he likes; let all behave as they like; we are in a free country, why should we not wipe our mouths upon the tablecloth if we please? Others again, devour books of etiquette on the quiet; they are very much in want of instruction as every one knows, but they have not the courage to confess that they are aware of this want, and are trying to pick up some knowledge of this kind to be useful to them; as their aim is to rise in the social scale, they would not let their friends know for worlds about this new study, but they know it, and find that they have improved, that they do not commit as many *gaucheries* as heretofore; still, they have caught the letter rather than the spirit of etiquette, they have read the rules it prescribes, and act up to them as far as their memories serve them; but they have failed in one essential particular of understanding that courtesy, consideration towards others, and unselfishness, are the sources of true politeness from which etiquette springs.

There is an idea amongst some few people who have mixed little in the world, and moved but in one fixed groove, that the more exalted the sphere, the more perfect the manners. It is needless to attempt to refute such a fallacy as this, for examples of the most perfect manner are to be met with not only amongst those who can boast of long lineage and high birth, but also amongst those who lay claim to neither.

Our present code of etiquette is constructed upon the refinement, polish, and culture of years, of centuries. Wealth and luxury, and contact with all that is beautiful in art and nature, have in all ages exercised a powerful influence on the manners of men; we do not say on the times, as unfortunately these advantages did not reach down to the many but were confined to the strictly few; but in these modern days the many have come, and still come, within the charmed circle; the ring broadens, ever widens; it is not now as in olden days that "their lot forbade." On the contrary, the possession of wealth or of talent is the open sesame to the most refined and cultured circles. The word etiquette is too narrow for all it embraces; it must be viewed in a double light, and be taken from a moral point as well as from a conventional one. A kindly nature, and an unselfish spirit are never wanting in true politeness, but the conventionalities of society give the finish and completeness to the whole, the colour, as it were, to the picture. In some the conventional spirit is uppermost and they have at best but a surface polish. In others the kindly feelings of the heart are allowed full play, and no act of genuine politeness is omitted or left undone in their intercourse with their fellows, and these graces of kindly politeness linger in the memory, trivial though they may have been, years after one has lost sight of this true gentleman or thorough lady, and one says of him, "What a charming man he was, how courteous and considerate, and how kind!" and of her, "She was the sweetest and prettiest-mannered woman I ever met."

It is only given to the very few to be thoroughly and unaffectedly charming without a shadow of self-consciousness or effort. To assume a would-be charming manner for the moment, with the desire to be unusually pleasing to some one in particular, does not confer the enviable reputation of having a charming manner. It does not sit easy enough to be altogether natural; it conveys the idea of being put on for the occasion, and, like all other imitations, it hardly ever pleases and seldom deceives. Etiquette and true politeness would have us go further than this, and our manners of to-day should be our manners of to-morrow, and not variable according to place and persons. The world is quick to note these uncertain demeanours, and every one's measure is readily taken and retained.

The rules of etiquette are indispensable to the smooth working of society at large. Take, for example, the etiquette of precedency, in force both in public and in private: on every public occasion, and in every private circle, precedency steps in to render assistance, and is as necessary in the smallest private circle as in the largest public gathering, because it assigns to every one his or her place as far as claim can be laid to place. Mistakes in the matter of precedency are not only committed by those who have enjoyed few social advantages, but by those also who have had everything in their favour. Young ladies, for instance, when married from the schoolroom, as it were, often make grave mistakes on the question of precedency, if they do not ignore it altogether.

The etiquette of card leaving and that of paying calls are indisputably necessary and only the very ignorant would attempt to gainsay their utility; without these aids to order and method all intercourse between friends and acquaintances would be uncertain and chaotic; as it is there is little excuse when the right thing is not done, and any departure from the simple rules laid down on these heads, is the best possible proof of the standing, position, and associations of the one at fault.

Any one point of etiquette if brought to the bar of common-sense would be pronounced reasonable, proper, and sensible; and there is strictly speaking no question of etiquette that cannot be thus judged and upon which a like verdict would not be given. There is no one rule of etiquette that can be described as absurd or ridiculous, arbitrary or tyrannical, and taken collectively the rules are but social obligations due from one person to another. Why should we not be a well-mannered people? Why should we not be refined, cultivated, and polished in our demeanour and bearing? Why should we not seek to charm if we can? Why should we not cultivate and encourage in ourselves consideration, thoughtfulness, and graciousness towards others in the smallest details of daily life?

CHAPTER II

THERE are ceremonious introductions and unceremonious introductions, premeditated introductions and unpremeditated introductions; but, in all cases, introductions should never be indiscriminately made — that is to say, without a previous knowledge on the part of those making them as to whether the persons thus introduced will be likely to appreciate each other, or the reverse, or unless they have expressed a desire to become acquainted. For instance, a lady should not introduce two of her acquaintances residing in a country town or watering-place, moving in different circles, unless they have each expressed such a desire.

An Undesired Introduction, if made, compels the one to whom it is the most unwelcome, to treat the other with marked coldness, or to continue an acquaintance that is distasteful.

Should the slightest doubt exist as to how an introduction will be received—whether the meditated introduction is a spontaneous desire on the part of a lady or gentleman, or whether one person expressed a wish to make the acquaintance of another person and expressed that wish to a mutual friend—the received rule is to consult the wishes of both persons on the subject before making the introduction.

When a Difference of Rank exists between two persons, it would be sufficient to ascertain the wishes of the person of highest rank alone.

A person about to make an introduction, should say to the one lady, but not in the hearing of the other, "Mrs. A——, may I introduce Mrs. B—— to you?" or some such formula, according to the degree of intimacy existing between herself and Mrs. A. (See "The Art of Conversing.")

When two ladies are of equal rank, the wishes of the person with whom the person making the introduction is least intimate should be consulted.

In the case of one person having expressed a wish to make the acquaintance of another, there remains but the wishes of one person to ascertain.

Acquiescence having been given, the introduction should be made.

In making an introduction, the lady of lowest rank should be introduced to the lady of highest rank; in no case should the lady of highest rank be introduced to the lady of lowest rank. This point of etiquette should always be strictly observed.

A Gentleman should always be introduced to a Lady, whatever his rank may be, without reference to her rank, whatever it may be. This rule is invariable, and is based upon the privilege of the sex—"*place aux dames.*"

It is not usual to ascertain a gentleman's wishes as to whether he will be introduced to a lady or not, although at a ball it is usual to do so when the introduction is made for a special object, viz., that of obtaining a partner for a lady; and as a gentleman may be either unable or unwilling to ask the lady to dance, it is incumbent to ascertain beforehand whether the introduction is desired or not, otherwise the introduction would be of no avail for the purpose, and prove a disappointment to the lady.

"Would you like to be introduced to Miss A——?" or some such polite phrase (see "The Art of Conversing"), is the sort of formula by which to ascertain a gentleman's wishes as to an introduction in the ball-room; as ball-room introductions are understood to mean an intention on the part of a gentleman to ask a lady to dance or to take her in to supper.

In general society, gentlemen are supposed to seek, rather than to avoid the acquaintance of ladies, irrespective of whatever sets in society to which they belong. It is immaterial to a gentleman in which set in society his acquaintances move, and he can be polite to all without offending any in their several circles.

With regard to his own sex a gentleman is generally as exclusive as to the acquaintanceships which he forms, as is a lady with regard to the acquaintanceships which she forms. Reciprocity of taste is the basis on which acquaintanceships between men are established, subject, in a certain measure, to social position; though this rule is itself subject to wide exceptions.

It is the rule for a gentleman to ask a mutual friend, or an acquaintance, for an introduction to a lady, and it is the received rule to do so when a gentleman desires to be introduced to any lady in particular; but gentlemen do not ask to be introduced to each other, unless some special reason exists for so doing—some reason that would commend itself to the person whose acquaintance was desired, as well as to the person making the introduction; otherwise, such a wish would appear to be either puerile or sycophantic, thus the request might meet with a refusal, and the proferred acquaintanceship be declined.

When Introductions are made between Ladies, an unmarried lady should be introduced to a married lady, unless the unmarried lady is of a higher rank than the married lady, when the rule is reversed.

The correct formula in use when making introductions is " Mrs. X——, Lady Z.," thus mentioning the name of the lady of lowest rank first, as she is the person introduced to the lady of highest rank. "Mrs. X——, Lady Z.," is all that need be said on the occasion by the person making the introduction. When the ladies are of equal rank it is immaterial which name is mentioned first; but there generally exists sufficient difference in the social position of the two ladies to give a slight distinction in favour of the one or of the other, which the person making the introduction should take into consideration.

When the introduction has been made, the ladies should bow to each other, and either lady should make a slight remark.

It is not usual for ladies on being first introduced to each other to shake hands, but only to bow; but there are very many exceptions to this rule.

When one lady is of higher rank than the other, should she offer to shake hands, it would be a compliment and a mark of friendliness on her part.

When a person introduces two intimate friends of his or hers to each other, they would be expected to shake hands, instead of bowing only.

The relations of an engaged couple should, on being introduced, shake hands with both bride and bridegroom elect, as should the intimate friends of an engaged couple ; as also should the relations of the two families on being introduced to each other.

It is the privilege of the lady to be the first to offer to shake hands, in every case, when a gentleman is introduced to her.

A lady should shake hands with every one introduced to her in her own house—that is to say, whether the person is brought by a mutual friend, or is present by invitation obtained through a mutual friend.

At Dinner-parties, both small and large, the hostess should use her own discretion as to the introductions she thinks proper to make. It is not customary to make general introductions at a dinner-party; but in sending guests down to dinner, who are strangers to each other, the host or hostess should introduce the gentleman to the lady whom he is to take down to dinner. It would be quite unnecessary to ask the lady's permission before doing so. It would be sufficient to make the introduction a few moments before dinner was announced, and the usual formula is, "Mrs. A., Mr. B. will take you in to dinner." A bow is the recognition of this introduction.

When the majority at a dinner-party are strangers to each other, a host or hostess should introduce one or two of the principal guests to each other, when time allows of its being done before dinner is served; such introductions are oftener made at country dinner-parties than at town dinner-parties.

A hostess should, in some instances, introduce ladies to each other in the drawing-room after dinner if the opportunity offers, and she considers it advisable to do so.

As a rule, a host seldom introduces gentlemen to each other in the dining-room after dinner, as they address each other as a matter of course on such occasions.

A hostess should introduce her principal guests to each other, at five-o'clock teas, garden-parties, small "at homes," etc.—that is to say, gentlemen to ladies—for the purpose of their taking the ladies to the tea-room. In this case also, the introduction should be made without previously consulting the lady; and a gentleman, knowing the reason of the introduction, should at once proffer the expected civility.

At these gatherings a hostess should use her own discretion as to any general introductions she thinks proper to make, and should introduce any gentleman to any lady without previously consulting the lady if she thinks the introduction will prove agreeable to her.

When introducing ladies to each other, she should give married ladies, and ladies of rank, the option of the

introduction; but should introduce young unmarried ladies
to each other if she thinks proper.

When Callers arrive simultaneously, the hostess
should introduce them directly or indirectly to each other,
if there is no social reason to the contrary.

When a hostess is aware that her visitors do not desire
each other's acquaintanceship, or, if she considers that the
introduction is not altogether a suitable one, agreeable to
both persons, she should not make it, but converse with
each visitor in turn, at the same time not allowing the
conversation to become too general.

At large gatherings, persons desirous of avoiding each
other's acquaintanceship, could be present at the house of
a mutual acquaintance without coming into direct contact
with one another, providing the host and hostess possessed
sufficient tact and discretion not to attempt to effect a
rapprochement between them.

At Country-house Parties, the hostess should introduce the principal ladies to one another on the first day of
their arrival; but if it is a large party, introductions should
not be generally made, but should be made according to the
judgment of the hostess. The fact of persons being guests
in the same house constitutes in itself an introduction, and
it rests with the guests thus brought together whether the
acquaintanceship ripens into subsequent intimacy or not.

The same remark applies in a degree to afternoon teas
and "at homes." The guests converse with each other if
inclined to do so. The act of so conversing would not
constitute an acquaintanceship, although it might, under
some circumstances, establish a bowing acquaintanceship,
especially between gentlemen.

Ladies should not bow to each other after only exchang-
ing a few remarks at afternoon tea, or at a garden-party,
unless there were some particular social link between them

to warrant their so doing, in which case the lady of highest rank should take the initiative.

Introductions at Public Balls.—It is erroneous to suppose that it is the duty of stewards to make introductions at public balls; it is the exception, and not the rule, for stewards to introduce persons to each other who are strangers to themselves.

Society objects, and the stewards object, to making promiscuous introductions, on the following grounds: first, as regards the chaperon, whether mother or relative, who has the charge of a young lady; then as regards a young lady herself; and last, but not least, as regards the position occupied by the steward himself. A chaperon naturally looks and feels displeased when a steward who is a stranger to herself offers to introduce a man who is evidently a stranger to him, which fact she gathers by his saying, "This gentleman wishes to be introduced to your daughter," or by his asking the stranger his name before making the introduction. A chaperon is responsible for the acquaintances a young lady forms while under her charge at a ball, and if amongst her own friends and acquaintances she cannot find partners for her, she would prefer that she spent a comparatively dull evening than that she should run the risk of forming undesirable acquaintances.

Young ladies have not always the discretion possessed by their elders, or sufficient knowledge of the world to do the right thing. Thus, some young ladies would either coldly decline the introductions, or if the introductions were made, would as coldly decline to dance, whilst others, anxious to dance, would accept both the introductions and the partners, and take their chance as to whether their brothers would like to see them dancing with strangers thus introduced. A steward himself particularly dislikes to be made responsible for a man he does not know; and whether a chaperon and a young lady are old friends of his, or whether they are merely new acquaintances, they equally trust to his not introducing men to them whom they would not care to know, and of whom he knows nothing save that they have solicited an introduction to them.

Very few stewards care to accost a lady whom they merely know by sight and by name for the purpose of introducing a stranger; they prefer to decline to make the introduction, on the plea of not having the honour of the lady's acquaintance.

Stewards consider that the position of a young man must be a peculiar one, and his presence at a ball somewhat of an anomaly, if he does not possess an acquaintance in the room, through whom he can become known to one or other of the stewards, or through whom he can be introduced to any particular lady with whom he may desire to dance.

When a gentleman is introduced to a young lady at a public ball, it generally means that he is introduced to her as a partner, and that though he may not ask her for the next dance, he will for a subsequent one, or that he will at least offer to take her in to supper, or, if earlier in the evening, to give her some tea, or if she declines these civilities, that he will continue a conversation with her until the next dance commences, or until a dance is over. When a gentleman does neither of these things, but walks away as soon as the introduction is made, it is a proof how little he desired it, and that doubtless the option was not given him of refusing it.

Good-natured friends of both sexes know how difficult it is to get partners for well-dressed, well-mannered, good-looking girls at a ball, unless they are more than ordinarily attractive in some way or other, in which case they are popular and sought after, and the only difficulty rests with the young ladies themselves as to how they shall best apportion the dances so as to satisfy their numerous partners, or persuade their chaperons to stay for one more dance which they have promised to, etc.

It is a well-known fact in the ball-going world that the majority of young men insist upon being introduced to the most popular girls in a ball-room, and refuse being introduced to one who does not appear to have plenty of partners.

Public balls are in reality made up of a number of small parties and different sets, each set or party being entirely independent of the other.

At county balls the county people take large houseparties, and each house-party does or does not mingle with other house-parties, according to standing or inclination.

If three large house-parties join forces at a ball they form a very imposing majority; but there are other sets in the same ball-room, dancing to the same band and adjourning to the same supper-room, equally apart and equally distinct.

At balls held at watering-places, although the residents do not take large house-parties, yet they join forces with those residents with whom they are acquainted, reinforced by friends who come down purposely to be present at the ball. Thus, on the face of it, a steward's introductions cannot fail to be ill-received, in whatever set he may be coerced into making them; and it is well understood that introductions, to prove acceptable, should only be made through friends and acquaintances, and even then with tact and judgment.

As the stewards of a ball are usually the most influential gentlemen in the place, it naturally follows that they are acquainted with many, if not with all, of the principal people present, therefore when they make introductions it is not by virtue of their office, but simply as a matter of friendship, and through being personally acquainted with those introduced by them.

Introductions out of doors are rather a matter of inclination than not, as, for instance, when a lady is walking with another lady to whom she is on a visit she should introduce any friends to her hostess she might happen to meet, and her hostess should do likewise if time and opportunity offer for so doing; should any reason exist for not making an introduction on the part of either lady, it should be explained when they are again alone, as were either of the ladies to exclude the other from the conversation it would be considered discourteous towards the one excluded. When two ladies accidentally meet when out walking, and are subsequently joined by two or more ladies, introductions should not be made by either of the ladies, unless some special reason exists for so doing. A lady, as a rule, should not introduce gentlemen to each other unless one of them is her host, when it would be correct to do so.

How to act on the Occasion of an Introduction is determined almost entirely upon the reason for its being made, and by whom and to whom the person is introduced. Even the *locale* has something to do with it, and thus a variety of issues are raised, upon which an instantaneous judgment has to be given. The mind has to travel with lightning rapidity over the ground to arrive at a correct course of action; but the mind does not always respond to the call made upon it : it hesitates, and acts not upon the outcome of reflection, but upon the spur of the moment.

The Received Rule is not to shake hands, but merely to bow on being introduced; but this rule under certain circumstances would not meet the case ; it would disappoint the one introducing and the one introduced. For instance if a relative of the former is the person introduced a bow would be a very chilling response to the introduction made; to shake hands, on the contrary, would be the correct thing to do, and both persons should offer at the same moment this cordial recognition. On the other hand, if a casual introduction is made without any premeditation, and those introduced are totally unknown to each other, an exchange of bows is all that is required of them.

Amongst the Exceptions for not merely bowing on being introduced are the introductions made between young ladies and elderly ones, and between young ladies themselves. An elderly lady, as a general rule, shakes hands with a girl introduced to her with the idea of being cordial and kind, not to say condescending, and girls generally shake hands with each other in place of bowing, as acquaintanceships formed by them have not the importance that attaches to those of older ladies ; besides, a greater readiness to make friends is the privilege and characteristic of youth.

Men take very much the Same View as regards introductions as do women—that is to say, if an introduction is made by a relative of the man introduced, the men would shake hands and not merely bow. This holds equally good where intimate friends are concerned : they almost rank on the footing of relations, and a cordial reception is given to an introduction thus made. When casual introductions are made of necessity rather than of intention men do not shake hands. When " I think you have met A." or " I think you know Mr. A." is said—the one by a host and the other by a hostess—nothing further is required from either than a bow and a smile of acquiescence accepting the introduction and a disclaimer is not expected if " Mr. A." is not actually known. The uncertainty is an excuse for making the introduction.

Ladies do not rise from their Seats on being introduced either at an " At Home " or before dinner is announced, or after dinner, or when calling when people are introduced to them, or when they themselves are introduced. Half an exception occurs, it is true, at crowded " at homes," when to rise and talk to the lady introduced is almost a necessity : there is no vacant seat for her to take, and, therefore, if both do not stand, conversation is at a deadlock, as the few first conventional remarks made by either are lost in the general buzz going on around ; also, it is awkward and ungraceful for a lady to bend over one seated for the purpose of saying a few platitudes. "Introductory remarks," or remarks following upon introductions, have too often a melancholy ring of commonplaceness about them and are distinctly trite. How can they be otherwise ? To venture out of the commonplace into originality would be suspicious of eccentricity, and no one wishes to be considered a little odd.

Before and after Dinner, when Introductions are made between ladies it is to those seated near to each other, and, therefore, there would be no occasion to rise, as there might be at an "at home." There is no question of a lady rising from her seat when a man is introduced to her, unless that man is her host, when she should rise and shake hands with him, or a clerical dignity—a bishop for instance, if opportunity allows of it, and on a semi-official occasion. This question does not trouble men, as they are usually found standing, or they are brought up to a person to be introduced, and even if a man ventures upon sitting down at an "at home," or before dinner is announced, he springs to his feet with alacrity when any approach is made in the matter of introducing him to a fellow guest.

Introductions often have to be made at Afternoon Calls, supposing that two or three callers only are present and the hostess feels that she must render the talk general by making some kind of introduction, direct or indirect, as she thinks best. The ladies thus introduced remain seated and bow. They do not shake hands even under the exceptional conditions previously referred to, but they would at once join in the talk that passes for conversation, and on departure would shake hands with the relative in question after having shaken hands with the hostess and having expressed pleasure at meeting this near relative— mother or sister, or whoever she may happen to be.

Introductions between Callers made under enforced circumstances have not much bearing on future acquaintance. Those introduced pass so short a time in each other's company, and know practically nothing of each other's surroundings, that they are uncertain whether at future meetings they ought to recollect that such introductions have taken place, and whether they should bow or forget. Actually it would be correct to bow if the opportunity is given so to do, but unless the wish to bestow recognition is mutual it is of little avail if grudgingly given, and it would be worse still were it withheld. Some people have short memories for faces, and others are short-sighted, and both these drawbacks have to be reckoned with when expecting recognition from a person to whom one has been thus introduced.

CHAPTER III

THE etiquette of card-leaving is a privilege which society places in the hands of ladies to govern and determine their acquaintanceships and intimacies, to regulate and decide whom they will, and whom they will not visit, whom they will admit into their friendship, and whom they will keep on the most distant footing, whose acquaintance they wish further to cultivate and whose to discontinue.

It would seem that the act of leaving cards is but imperfectly understood, and that many erroneous impressions prevail respecting the actual use of visiting cards. The object of leaving cards is to signify that a call has been made, due civility shown, and a like civility expected in return.

Leaving cards, or card-leaving, is one of the most important of social observances, as it is the ground-work or nucleus in general society of all acquaintanceships. Leaving cards, according to etiquette, is the first step towards forming, or towards enlarging, a circle of acquaintances, and the non-fulfilment of the prescribed rules is a sure step in the opposite direction. The following is the received code of card-leaving in all its details according to the etiquette observed in good society by both ladies and gentlemen, and should be faithfully followed.

A Lady's Visiting Card should be printed in small, clear copper-plate script, and free from any kind of embellishment as regards ornamental or Old English letters. It should not be a thin card, and should be three inches and five eighths in width, and slightly under two and a half in depth.

The name of the lady should be printed in the centre of the card, and her address in the left-hand corner. If she has a second address, it should be printed in the opposite corner of the card. If the second address is but a temporary one, it is usually written and not printed.

A married lady should never use her christian name on a card, but she should use her husband's christian name before her surname if his father or elder brother is living.

It is now considered old-fashioned for husbands and wives to have their names printed on the same card, although at watering-places, the practice of having the two names on the same card, " Mr. and Mrs. Dash," is still occasionally followed ; but even when these cards are used, a lady and gentleman still require separate cards of their own.

A lady having a large acquaintance should keep a visiting book, in which to enter the names of her acquaintances, and the date when their cards were left upon her, with the dates of her return cards left upon them, that she might know whether a card were due to her from them, or whether it were due to them from her.

A lady having a small acquaintance would find a memorandum book sufficient for the purpose ; a line should be drawn down the centre of every page, dividing it into two columns, the one column for the names, and the opposite column for the dates of the calls made and returned.

Leaving cards principally devolves upon the mistress of a house ; a wife should leave cards for her husband, as well as for herself ; and a daughter for her father. The master of a house has little or no card-leaving to do, beyond leaving cards upon his bachelor friends.

In the country it is otherwise, and those who return

home are called upon by their friends and acquaintances in the first instance, unless under exceptional circumstances.

Ladies arriving in town should leave cards on their acquaintances and friends to intimate that they have returned.

Visiting cards should be left in person, and should not be sent by post, although in town, when the distance is considerable, it is tacitly allowed; but, as a rule, ladies invariably leave their cards themselves. On arriving in town for the season ladies having a large acquaintance often send their visiting cards to their various friends and acquaintances by a manservant or through a stationer.

The Routine of Card-leaving.—As regards the routine of card-leaving. When driving, a lady should desire her footman to inquire if the mistress of the house at which she is calling is " at home." If not " at home," and it is a first call, she should hand him *three* cards—*one* of her own, and *two* of her husband's. Her card is left for the mistress of the house, and her husband's cards for both master and mistress.

If not a first call a lady should leave one only of her husband's cards if his acquaintance with her friend's husband is an intimate one and they are in the habit of meeting frequently. If, on the contrary, they know each other but slightly, and meet but seldom, then two of his cards should be left. This, however, not on every occasion of calling.

When a lady is merely leaving cards, she should hand the three cards to her servant, saying, " For Mrs. ——." This ensures the cards being left at the right address, and is the correct formula for the occasion.

When a lady is walking, and finds the mistress of the house at which she calls is "not at home," she should act as above.

When a lady intends making a call she should ask if

C

"Mrs. —— is at home?" And if the answer is in the affirmative, she should, after making the call, leave *two* of her husband's cards on the hall table, and neither put them in the card-basket nor leave them on the drawing-room table, nor offer them to her hostess, all of which would be very incorrect; but she might on reaching the hall hand them to the manservant silently, or she might send them in by her own servant when seated in her carriage, saying, "For Mr. and Mrs. Smith." She should not leave her *own* card on the hall table, as, having seen the lady of the house, the reason for doing so no longer exists.*

When a lady calling is accompanied by her husband and the mistress of the house is at home, the husband should leave one of his cards only, for the absent master of the house; when the master of the house is at home also, a card in that case should not be left.

When the mistress of a house has a grown-up daughter or daughters, the lady leaving cards should turn down one corner of her visiting card—the right-hand corner gene-rally—to include the daughter or daughters in the call. This custom of turning down a corner of a visiting card signifies that other ladies of the family besides the hostess are included in the call. A foreigner turns down the *end* of a card instead of one corner only, which has not the same signification. It is to denote that he has left it in person.

A lady should not leave one of her husband's cards for the daughters of the house, but she not unfrequently leaves his card for the grown-up sons of the house.

When a lady intends leaving cards on a friend who is the guest of some one with whom she is unacquainted, she should only leave cards for her friend and not for her friend's hostess; but if she is slightly acquainted with her

---

* It is, however, permissible on the occasion of a *first* call to say, "I shall leave my card in the hall to remind you of my address"; or some such phrase.

friend's hostess, she should leave cards upon her on the occasion of her first visit to her friend, but it would not be necessary to do so at every subsequent visit, especially if they were of frequent occurrence.

Young ladies should not have visiting cards of their own; their names should be printed beneath that of their mother on her card. In the case of there being no mother living, the daughter's name should be printed beneath that of her father on the usual lady's visiting card, but never on the smaller cards used by gentlemen. When young ladies are taken out into society by relatives or friends, their names should be written in pencil under the names of the ladies chaperoning them on their visiting cards.

Maiden ladies of a certain age should have visiting cards of their own, but until a young lady has attained what is termed a certain age, it argues no little independence of action to have a card of her own; but when she no longer requires chaperonage, she is entitled to a card of her own, being clearly her own mistress, and able to choose her own acquaintances.

When a young lady is on a visit unaccompanied by her parents, and wishes to call on ladies with whom the lady she is staying with is unacquainted, she should leave her mother's card on which her own name is also printed, and should draw a pencil through her mother's name to intimate that she was not with her on that occasion.

Cards should always be returned within a week if possible, or ten days at latest, after they have been left, but to do so within a week is more courteous. And care must be taken to return the "call" or "cards" according to the etiquette observed by the person making the call or leaving the card; that is to say, that a "call" must *not* be returned by a card only, or a "card" by a "call." This is a point ladies should be very punctilious about.

Should a lady of higher rank return a card by a "call," asking if the mistress of the house were "at home," her so doing would be in strict etiquette; and should she return a "call" by a card only, it should be understood that she wished the acquaintance to be of the slightest; and should a lady call upon an acquaintance of higher rank than herself, who had only left a card upon her, her doing so would be a breach of etiquette.

In large establishments the hall porter enters the names of all callers in a book expressly kept for the purpose, while some ladies merely desire their servant to sort the cards left for them.

The name of the lady or gentleman for whom the cards are intended should never be written on the cards left at a house. The only case in which it should be done would be when cards are left on a lady or a gentleman staying at a crowded hotel, when, to save confusion, and to ensure their receiving them, their names should be written on them thus: "For Mr. and Mrs. Smith." But this would be quite an exceptional case, otherwise to do so would be extremely vulgar.

Leaving Cards after Entertainments. —Visiting

cards should be left after the following entertainments: balls, receptions, private theatricals, amateur concerts, and dinners, by those who have been invited, whether the invitations have been accepted or not, and should be left the day after the entertainment if possible, and certainly within the week according to the rules of card-leaving already described. On these occasions cards should be left without inquiry as to whether the hostess is at home, although after a dinner-party it is the rule to ask if she is at home, as to dine at a house denotes a greater intimacy than being present at a large gathering. If the hostess were not at home, cards should be left.

If a lady has been but once present at any entertainment, whether the invitation came through a mutual friend or direct from the hostess herself, the hostess being but a slight acquaintance of her own, besides leaving cards on her the day following, she can, if she desires, leave cards on her the following season, or, if residing in the same town, within a reasonable time of the entertainment; but if these cards are not acknowledged by cards being left in return, she should of course understand that the acquaintance is to proceed no further.

A lady should not leave cards on another lady to whom she has but recently been introduced at a dinner-party or afternoon tea; for instance, she must meet her several times in society, and feel sure that her acquaintance is desired, before venturing to leave cards. If two ladies are of equal rank, tact will be their best guide as to the advisability of leaving cards or not upon each other; the lady of superior rank may take the initiative if she pleases. If either of the ladies express a wish to further the acquaintance by asking the other to call upon her, the suggestion should come from the lady of highest rank; if of equal rank it is immaterial as to which first makes the suggestion. But in either case the call should be paid within the week.

Leaving Cards upon New-comers.—In the country the residents should be the first to leave cards on the new-comers, after ascertaining the position which the new-comers occupy in society.

Persons moving in the same sphere should either leave cards or call according as they intend to be ceremonious or friendly, and the return visits should be paid in like manner, a card for a card, a call for a call.

It is the received rule that residents should call on new-comers, although having no previous acquaintance with them, or introductions to them.

New-comers, even if of higher rank, should not call on residents in the first instance, but should wait until the residents have taken the initiative. If residents do not wish to continue the acquaintance after the first meeting, it is discontinued by not leaving cards, or by not calling again, and if the new-comers feel disinclined to continue the acquaintance they should return the calls by leaving cards only. Calling on new-comers in the country should not be done indiscriminately, and due consideration should be paid to individual status in society.

The lady of highest social position in the circle to which the new-comers belong generally takes the responsibility of calling first on the new-comers. By new-comers is expressed persons who intend to reside in a county or town for a long, or even for a short period, and who are not casual visitors in the place.

The custom of residents calling on new-comers is entirely confined to county society, and does not apply to residents in large towns and populous watering-places.

In old cathedral cities and quiet country towns, far from the metropolis, on the contrary, the rule holds good of residents calling on new-comers.

Cards " To Inquire."—Cards to inquire after friends during their illness should be left in person, and should not be sent by post; but they may be sent by a servant. On a lady's visiting card should be written above the printed name: " To inquire after Mrs. Smith." When the person inquired after is sufficiently recovered to return thanks in person, the usual visiting card, with " many thanks for kind inquiries," written above the printed name, is the usual mode of returning thanks, and is all-sufficient for the purpose.

P.P.C. Cards.—Formerly P.P.C. cards were left within a week of departure, or within ten days if the acquaintance was a large one.

The letters P.P.C. for *pour prendre congé*, written at the lower corner of visiting cards, indicate departure from town or from a neighbourhood. P.P.C. cards may be left in person or sent by a servant; they can also be sent by post. The object of leaving P.P.C. cards is to avoid leave-takings and correspondence concerning departure, and to prevent offence being given if letters and invitations remained unanswered.

In the country an absence of from three to six months renders leaving P.P.C. cards somewhat necessary ; under that period it would be unnecessary to give notice of a temporary absence which does not amount to an actual departure. Short absences render it unnecessary to leave P.P.C. cards. Holiday movements at Christmas, Easter, and Whitsuntide are thoroughly recognized, and no leave-taking is obligatory. P.P.C. cards are now seldom if ever left in town.

Business Calls.—When a lady makes a strictly business call upon either a lady or gentleman she should give her card to the servant to be taken to his master or mistress, but on no other occasion should she do so.

Gentlemen's Visiting Cards.—A gentleman's card should be thin—thick cards are not in good taste—and not glazed, and of the usual narrow width, *i.e.* one and a half inches in depth, and three inches in width ; his name should be printed in the centre, thus : " Mr. Smith " or " Mr. Francis Smith," should he require the addition of his christian name to distinguish him from his father or elder brother. To have " Francis Smith " printed on the card without the prefix of " Mr." would be in bad taste.

Initials appertaining to honorary rank should never be written or printed on a card, such as D.L., Q.C., M.P., K.C.B., M.D., etc. Military or professional titles necessarily precede the surname of the person bearing them, and are always used, such as " Colonel Smith," " Captain Smith," " Reverend H. Smith," " Dr. Smith," etc.

As regards titles, " The Honourable " is the only title that is not used on a visiting card. Thus " The Honourable Henry Smith's " card should bear the words " Mr. Henry Smith " only.

A Baronet's card should be printed thus, "Sir George Smith," and a Knight's card thus, "Sir Charles Smith." A gentleman's address should be printed in the left hand corner of the card. If a member of a club, it is usual to print the name of the club at the right hand. Officers usually have the name of the club printed at the left hand corner in the place of the address, and the regiment to which they belong at the right hand.

Cards should be printed in small copper-plate script, without ornamentation of any kind. Old English letters look old-fashioned on a card, and are but little used; and ornamental capital letters are never used, and are out of date. The lettering should be as plain and as free from any sort of embellishment as it well can be.

The Routine of Card-leaving for Gentlemen.—

To bachelors card-leaving is an irksome routine of etiquette, and is, therefore, in a measure often neglected, by reason of their having little or no leisure at command during the afternoon hours. This is now thoroughly understood and accepted in general society. When, however, a bachelor has his way to make in society and has leisure to further the acquaintanceships he has already made, he should follow the rules of card-leaving.

Bachelors, as a rule, are expected to leave cards on the master and mistress of a house with whom they are acquainted as soon as they are aware that the family have arrived in town; or if a bachelor himself has been away, he should leave cards on his acquaintances immediately after his return. He should leave one card for the mistress of the house and one for its master.

A gentleman should not turn down a corner of his card, even though he may be acquainted with other ladies of the family besides the mistress of the house. A gentleman should not leave a card for the young daughters of the house, or for any young relative of its mistress who might be staying with her; but if a married couple with whom he is acquainted were staying with the friends on whom he is calling, he should leave two cards for them, one for the wife and one for the husband, and should tell the servant for whom they are intended.

As regards leaving cards upon new acquaintances, a gentleman should not leave his card upon a married lady, or the mistress of a house, to whom he has been introduced, however gracious or agreeable she has been to him, unless she expressly asks him to call, or gives him to understand in an unmistakable manner that his doing so would be agreeable to her. This rule holds good, whether the introduction has taken place at a dinner-party, at a ball, at an "at home," at a country-house gathering, or elsewhere; he would not be entitled to leave his card on her on such slight acquaintanceship; as, if she desired his further acquaintance, she would make some polite allusion to his calling at her house, in which case he should leave his card on her as soon afterwards as convenient, and he should also leave a card for the master of the house, the lady's husband or father (as the case may be), even if he had not made his acquaintance when making that of the lady.

A gentleman should not leave a card on a young lady to whom he has been introduced, but upon her mother or the relative with whom she is residing.

When the acquaintance existing between gentlemen is but slight, they should occasionally leave cards upon each other, especially when they do not move in the same circle, and are not otherwise likely to meet; it generally follows that the one who most desires the acquaintanceship is the one to leave his card first, always supposing that the strength of the acquaintance would warrant his so doing. The one of highest rank should be the one to intimate that he desires the acquaintance of the other; if the rank be equal, it is a matter of inclination which calls first.

The rules of etiquette, though stringent as regards

acquaintances, have little or no application as regards intimate friends ; friendship overrules etiquette.

When a bachelor has a number of intimate friends, very little card-leaving is required from him as far as they are concerned.

Leaving Cards after Entertainments.—In the event of a gentleman receiving an invitation to an entertainment from an acquaintance, or from a new acquaintance, or through some mutual friend, he should leave his cards at the house within a week or ten days after the entertainment, one for the mistress and one for the master of the house, whether he ·has accepted the invitation or not. Between friends this rule is greatly relaxed.

It is usual for a gentleman to leave his cards on the host or on the hostess, after every entertainment to which he has been invited by them, whether it be a dinner-party, or ball, or "at home," etc. Whether he has been present or not, the fact of his having been invited by them obliges him to pay them this civility, although great latitude as regards time is now accorded in general society with regard to this particular rule.

If invited by a new acquaintance, the cards should be left a few days after the entertainment, but if by a less recent acquaintance they should be left within ten days or a fortnight, but the earlier the cards are left the greater the politeness shown.

If a bachelor acquaintance gives an entertainment, the same rule applies as to the necessity of cards being left on him by those gentlemen but slightly acquainted with him who have been invited to the entertainment.

When a gentleman has been invited to an entertainment given at the house of a new acquaintance, whether the acquaintance be a lady or a gentleman, it would be etiquette for him to leave his card upon them on their arrival in town or elsewhere, even though they may not have invited him to any subsequent entertainment given by them within the year. If during the following year they do not again invite him, he might consider the acquaintance at an end and cease to call. These complimentary calls made, or rather cards left, should not average more than four during the year.

Memorial Cards are out of date in society, and consequently should not be sent to either relatives or friends.

A widow should not make use of her christian name on her visiting cards to distinguish her from other members of her late husband's family. Her cards should be printed as during his lifetime.

CHAPTER IV

LADIES stand upon strict and ceremonious etiquette with each other as regards both paying and receiving calls. Ignorance or neglect of the rules which regulate paying calls, brings many inconveniences in its train; for instance, when a lady neglects to pay a call due to an acquaintance, she runs the risk of herself and daughters being excluded from entertainments given by the said acquaintance.

When a call has not been made within a reasonable time, a coldness is apt to arise between ladies but slightly acquainted with each other. Some ladies take this omission good-naturedly or indifferently, while with others the acquaintance merges into a mere bowing acquaintance to be subsequently dropped altogether.

The first principle of calling is, that those who are the first to arrive in town should be the *first* to call upon their acquaintances to intimate their return.

"Morning calls," so designated on account of their being made before dinner, are, more strictly speaking, "afternoon calls," as they should only be made between the hours of three and six o'clock.

Calls made in the morning—that is before one o'clock —would not come under the denomination of "morning calls," as they can only be made by intimate friends and not by acquaintances, and are not, therefore, amenable to the rules of etiquette which govern the afternoon calls, which calls are regulated in a great measure—as to the hour of calling—by the exact degree of intimacy existing between the person who calls and the person called upon. From three to four o'clock is the ceremonious hour for calling; from four to five o'clock is the semi-ceremonious hour; and from five to six o'clock is the wholly friendly and without ceremony hour.

If a lady is driving when she calls at the house of an acquaintance, she should say to her servant, "Ask if Mrs. A—— is at home."

When a lady is walking, she should ask the same question herself.

When the answer is in the negative, she should leave one of her own cards and one of her husband's, and should say to the servant, "For Mr. and Mrs. A——."

When the answer is in the affirmative, the lady should enter the house without further remark and follow the servant to the drawing-room.

The servant should go before the visitor, to lead the way to the drawing-room, and, however accustomed a visitor may be to a house, it is still the proper etiquette for the servant to lead the way, and announce him or her to his mistress; and this rule should not be dispensed with, except in the case of very near relations or very intimate friends.

At the drawing-room door the servant waits for a moment until the visitor has reached the landing, when the visitor should give his or her name to the servant, "Mr. A——" or "Mrs. A——," should the servant be unacquainted with it.

If the visitor calling bears the title of "Honourable" it should not be mentioned by him or her to the servant when giving the name, neither should it be mentioned by the servant when announcing the visitor.

All titles are given in full by the servants of those who bear them, thus: "The Duke and Duchess of A——," "The Marquis and Marchioness of B——," "The Earl and Countess of C——," "Viscount and Viscountess D——," "Lord and Lady E——," etc.; but a marchioness, a countess, or a viscountess when giving her name to be announced at a morning call would style herself "Lady A——" only.

A gentleman or lady should never give his or her visiting card to the servant when the mistress of the house is at home.

A servant should not knock at the drawing-room door when announcing visitors. The servant, on opening the drawing-room door, should stand inside the doorway, he should not stand behind the door, but well into the room; facing the mistress of the house if possible, and should say, "Mr. A——," or "Mrs. A——."

When the mistress of the house is not in the drawing-room when a visitor arrives, the visitor should seat herself and rise at her entrance.

Visitors should not make any inquiries of the servant as to how long his mistress will be, or where she is, or what she is doing, etc. Visitors are not expected to converse with the servants of their acquaintances, and should not enter into conversation with them.

Formerly a gentleman when calling, took his hat and stick in his hand with him into the drawing-room, and held them until he had seen the mistress of the house and shaken hands with her. He either placed them on a chair or table near at hand or held them in his hand, according as to whether he felt at ease or the reverse, until he took his leave. Many middle-aged and elderly men still follow this fashion in a degree, and take their hats and sticks into the drawing-room when making formal calls.

The newer fashion amongst younger men is to leave their hats and sticks in the hall and not to take them into the drawing-room with them when calling. To do this is now very general, as hats are in the way if tea is going on;

besides, men were apt to forget where they placed their hats, and frequently had to return to the drawing-room in search of them.

At "at homes," small afternoon teas, luncheons, dinners, etc., the rule is the same, and hats are left in the hall by invited guests.

A gentleman should not take his stick or umbrella with him into the drawing-room, but leave it in the hall.

When gentlemen wear gloves, they can take them off or keep them on as they please, it is immaterial which they do, but when a call is made when tea is going on, it is more usual to take them off.

When the mistress of the house is in the drawing-room when a visitor is announced—and she should so arrange her occupations as always to be found there on the afternoons when she intends being "at home" should visitors call—she should rise, come forward, and shake hands with her visitor. She should not ask her visitor to be seated, or to "take a seat," but she might say, "Where will you sit?" or, "Will you sit here?" or something to this effect; and should at once sit down and expect her visitor to do the same, as near to herself as possible.

Both hostess and visitor should guard against displaying a fussy demeanour during a morning call, as a morning call is oftener than not a *tête-à-tête*, and a *tête-à-tête* between two persons but slightly acquainted with each other requires a considerable amount of tact and *savoir vivre* to be sustained with ease and self-possession. A fussy woman is without repose, without dignity, and without *savoir vivre*.

A hostess betrays that she is not much accustomed to society when she attempts to amuse her visitor by the production of albums, photographs, books, illustrated newspapers, portfolios of drawings, the artistic efforts of the members of the family, and the like; conversation being all that is necessary, without having recourse to pictorial displays.

If not intimate enough to refer to family matters, the conversation should turn on light topics of the hour.*

People unused to society are apt to fall back upon the above adventitious aids. A hostess should rely solely upon her own powers of conversation to make the short quarter of an hour—which is the limit of a ceremonious call—pass pleasantly to her visitor. The hostess should not offer her visitor any refreshments, wine and cake, for instance. No refreshments whatever, save tea, should be offered to morning visitors; they are not supposed to require them.

In the country it is customary to offer sherry to gentlemen callers, and to order tea for the ladies, even though the call is made rather early in the afternoon, and a little before the hour for having tea.

Ceremonious visits are usually paid before the hour of half-past four; but if tea is brought in while the visitor is in the drawing-room, or if the visitor calls while the hostess is having tea, she should naturally offer her visitor tea.

When the mistress of the house only expects a few callers, "tea" is placed on a small table—a silver tray being generally used for the purpose. The hostess should pour out the tea herself; when a gentleman is present, he should hand the cups to the visitors or visitor, otherwise the hostess should herself do so, and then hand the sugar and cream, without asking whether her visitors will have either, unless she is preparing the cups of tea herself, in which case she should ask the question.

When a second visitor arrives, ten or fifteen minutes after the first visitor, the first visitor should take her leave as soon as she conveniently can. When the second visitor is a lady, the hostess should rise and shake hands with her, and then seat herself; the first visitor, if a lady, should not rise; if a gentleman, he should do so.

A hostess should also rise and come forward when a gentleman is announced; this gives her an opportunity of

* See work entitled "The Art of Conversing."

talking to him for a few moments on his first entering the room. The second visitor should at once seat him or herself near to the hostess.

She should introduce the callers to each other unless she has some especial reason for not doing so. She could, however, in the course of conversation merely mention the name of each caller, so that each may become aware of the name of the other. This is now often done when formal introductions are not made. If the hostess possesses tact, and a facility and readiness of speech, she should skilfully draw both callers into the conversation (a subject which is fully enlarged upon in "The Art of Conversing"). The hostess should not take this latter course unless aware that the two visitors would be likely to appreciate each other.

When one visitor arrives immediately after the other, the hostess should converse equally with both visitors, and the lady who was the first to arrive should be the first to leave, after a call of from ten to fifteen minutes. When only one visitor is present the hostess should accompany her to the door of the drawing-room, and linger for a few moments, whilst the visitor is descending the stairs. To do so would not be imperative, but it would be courteous. When the host is present he should accompany the lady downstairs into the hall; this also is an optional civility, and greatly depends upon the estimation in which the lady is held by host and hostess.

When two visitors are present the hostess should rise and shake hands with the departing visitor; but unless a person of greater consideration than the visitor who still remained seated, she should not accompany her to the drawing-room door.

One visitor should not rise from her seat when another is about to take her leave. When visitors are acquainted with each other they should rise and shake hands. When one of the visitors is a gentleman he should rise, even if

D

unacquainted with the lady who is about to take her leave;
he should not remain seated when the hostess is standing.

When two visitors, either two ladies or two gentlemen,
have slightly conversed with each other during a morning
call, they should not shake hands with each other on
leaving, but should merely bow. When they have not
spoken to each other, they should not bow.

When they have been formally introduced they should
still only bow, unless the acquaintance has progressed into
sudden intimacy through previous knowledge of each other.

When one of the visitors present is a gentleman he
should open the drawing-room door for the departing
visitor, but he should not accompany her downstairs unless
requested by the hostess to do so; the visitor should bow
to him and thank him, but not shake hands with him.

When the hostess has shaken hands with a guest, and
before crossing the room with her, she should ring the
drawing-room bell, that the servant may be in readiness in
the hall to open the door and to call up the carriage. She
should ring the bell even if the host were accompanying
the lady downstairs. It would be thoughtless on the part
of the hostess to forget to ring the bell to give notice to
the servant that a visitor was leaving.

In the country, where sometimes the horses are taken
out of the carriage, the visitor before rising to depart should
ask if she might ring and order her carriage. When the
hostess is within reach of the bell, she should ring it for
her; when a gentleman is present, he should do so. On the
servant's entrance, the visitor should ask for her carriage.

When a lady is calling on a friend, the guest of some one
with whom she herself is unacquainted, or even but slightly
acquainted, she should in both cases ask if her friend is at
home, and not if the mistress of the house is at home; and
having paid her visit, on leaving the house she should leave
cards for its mistress if she is slightly acquainted with her,
but should not do so if she is unacquainted with her.

When a lady has a guest staying on a visit to her, if convenient, she should, when her guest expected visitors, absent herself from the drawing-room at that particular time, unless the expected visitors are mutual friends of herself and guest.

If she is in the drawing-room with her guests when a visitor is announced so as to render an introduction inevitable, a formal introduction should be made, but the mistress of the house, after a very few minutes, should make some excuse, quietly leave the room, and not return until after the departure of the visitor. It would be inconsiderate were the mistress of the house to remain in the drawing-room while calls were paid to her guest by strangers to herself unless at her guest's particular request. When a visitor is a gentleman, and the guest a young unmarried lady, the mistress of the house should remain in the drawing-room to chaperon her.

When the mistress of the house is desirous of making the acquaintance of any particular friend of her guest, from whom she expected a visit, when the visit occurs and previous to the visitor taking her leave, the guest should ask if she will allow her to introduce her to the lady with whom she is staying. If her visitor desires the introduction, she should then ring and request the servant to tell his mistress that Mrs. A. is in the drawing-room, which message the hostess would understand to mean that her presence is desired, and the introduction would then be made on her appearing. An introduction, if made in this manner, could become the basis of a future acquaintance, both ladies having had the option of refusing the acquaintance of the other if so disposed; whereas a forced introduction where no option is given would hardly count as the basis of a future acquaintance unless the ladies thus introduced mutually appreciated each other.

In the country a guest seldom has friends and acquaintances in the neighbourhood, who are unknown to her hostess; if otherwise, the hostess should give her guest the opportunity of seeing her visitor by leaving them together when the call is made.

When a guest is present when the mistress of a house is receiving callers, she should introduce them to her guest or her guest to them, according to the rank of either (see Chapter II.).

When a lady is driving with a friend who is a stranger to the acquaintance on whom she is calling, she should not take her into the house with her while she makes her call, unless she is a young lady, or unless there is some especial reason for introducing the two ladies to each other, or unless both ladies have expressed a wish to become acquainted with each other. Husbands and wives occasionally pay calls together, but oftener they do not. A lady, as a rule, pays a call by herself, unless she has a grown-up daughter, when she should accompany her mother.

Occasionally two ladies, both intimate with the lady of the house, pay their calls together. A family party, of father and mother and daughter, or daughters, rarely call in town together, save under very exceptional circumstances; but in the country a family party of three or four would, as a matter of course, call together; it is country etiquette to do so.

A considerable difference exists with regard to "Sunday calls," or calling on Sundays. Ladies should not pay ceremonious calls on Sundays; it would not be etiquette for an acquaintance to call on a Sunday, it would rather be considered a liberty, unless she were expressly asked to do so. Intimate friends, on the contrary, often make Sunday a special day for calling, and therefore, ladies and gentlemen —more especially gentlemen—extend their calling hours from three until six o'clock on Sundays.

When a lady is acquainted with the daughters of a family only, and not with their father or mother, she should call on the daughters, who should at once introduce her to their mother on the next occasion of calling. If the mother is not present, the lady calling should leave cards for her; and at all morning calls, when the daughters of the house receive a ceremonious visit from an acquaintance, in the absence of their mother, whether from indisposition or any other cause, cards should be left for her in the hall before leaving by the lady calling (see Chapter III.).

In all cases, when "morning calls" are made, and the lady called on is not at home, cards should be left according to the etiquette described in Chapter II., an etiquette which should be strictly observed; when the lady called on is "at home," cards should be left for the gentlemen of the family, according to the same rules of card-leaving, which cannot be too punctiliously followed.

A mistress of a house should inform her servant after or before luncheon, or before the hours for calling, whether she intends to be "at home" to visitors or not during the afternoon.

"Not at home" is the understood formula expressive of not wishing to see visitors.

"Not at home" is not intended to imply an untruth, but rather to signify that for some reason, or reasons, it is not desirable to see visitors; and as it would be impossible to explain to acquaintances the why and the wherefore of its being inconvenient to receive visitors, the formula of "Not at home" is all-sufficient explanation, provided always that a servant is able to give a direct answer at once of "Not at home" when the query is put to him. If a servant is not sure as to whether his mistress wishes to see visitors or not, it is almost a direct offence to the lady calling if he hesitates as to his answer, and leaves her either sitting in her carriage or standing in the hall, while "He will see if his mistress is 'at home,'" perhaps returning with the unsatisfactory answer that she is "Not at home"; in which case the intimation is almost received as a personal exclusion rather than as a general exclusion of visitors.

If a lady is dressing to go out when a visitor calls, the servant can mention that fact to a visitor calling, and offer to ascertain if his mistress will see the caller; and the caller should use her own discretion as to whether she will allow him to do so or not; but unless the visit is one of importance, it would be best in such a case only to leave cards.

When a second visitor calls, a servant should not be permitted to say that his mistress is " engaged with a lady," or "with a gentleman," but should usher the second caller into the drawing-room, as he has previously done the first caller. He should not inquire as to whether his mistress will see the second caller or not. Neither should he inform the second caller as to whether any one is or is not with his mistress, as ignorant servants are too apt to do.

It is not usual to offer coffee at afternoon tea; tea only is given. To offer coffee is a foreign fashion, and not an English one.

"Morning" callers should not be conducted to the dining-room to have tea; and tea is only served in the dining-room on the occasion of a large afternoon tea, or afternoon "at home," etc. (See chapter on "Afternoon 'At Homes,'" p. 151.)

The tea hour varies from 4 to 4.30 o'clock. When callers are present at 4 o'clock, tea should be brought in at that hour. It should be placed upon a small table, which is first covered with a white linen or damask tea-cloth. The tea-tray should be large enough to hold, in addition to the china, silver teapot, etc., an urn for hot water, which should be brought in and placed upon it. A stand containing hot cakes, an uncut cake, small cakes, tiny sandwiches, and thin bread-and-butter should be placed near to the tea-table. Tiny tea-plates should be placed in a pile upon the tea-tray, they being in general use. The hostess or her daughter should pour out the tea.

Apart from the foregoing style of afternoon tea is the

newer fashion of what might be termed "a round-table tea," at which hostess and guests sit, but this style is more usual at country houses than in town houses at present, on account of the space required, if for no other reason. The tea is served in a smaller drawing-room, upon a large round or oval table, which is covered with a white table-cloth, upon which the tea-tray with all its contents is placed. Cakes, hot and cold, sandwiches, pastry, fruit, jam, bread-and-butter, biscuits, dry toast, etc., are given, and the visitors seated at the table help themselves to what they require. The hostess pours out the tea and hands the cups as when guests are not seated in this way. Dessert plates and dessert knives and forks should be placed on the table beside the small tea-plates, to be taken as required.

CHAPTER V

THE order of precedency due to each individual according to rank is a matter of great importance at official banquets and at ceremonious dinner-parties, when its correct observance should be strictly adhered to.

As regards Precedency amongst Royal Personages, the Sovereign takes precedence of all others in the realm; the King takes precedence of Queen Mary. The Prince of Wales takes precedence of the Duke of Connaught. Queen Alexandra takes precedence of the Royal Princesses. The Royal Princesses take precedence of their husbands, the Duke of Fife, Prince Christian, and the Duke of Argyll.

The Precedency accorded to Foreign Royal Personages in this country very much depends upon their individual rank. Imperial Highnesses and Royal Highnesses take precedence of Serene Highnesses.

The Precedency accorded to Eastern Princes is generally synonymous with that accorded to Serene Highnesses; but in some instances the claims of individual precedency are so difficult to define, that in official cases it is sometimes necessary to make a special rule as to the amount of precedency to be allowed.

As regards General Precedency it is, perhaps, needless to say archbishops take precedence of dukes, dukes take precedence of earls, earls take precedence of viscounts, and so on throughout the various degrees of nobility.

All Ambassadors, Ministers and Diplomatic Officers take precedence next after dukes, in the order of their seniority of service in England. In all cases where precedency is to be established between persons of equal rank it is necessary to refer to a Peerage for date of creation of title, as this actually decides all precedency.

For Precedency due to Baronets and their wives a Baronetage should be consulted.

For Precedency due to Knights and their wives a Knightage should be consulted in reference to each order of knighthood.

For the Precedency due to the Legal Profession a Law List should be consulted when it is not defined by office or birth.

For the Precedency due to the Clergy a Clergy List should be consulted when superior preferment or birth does not define it.

For the Precedency due to Officers in the army and navy an Army List and a Navy List should be consulted to determine the precedency due to each in the separate Services.

Officers should be sent in to Dinner according to the dates of commission, but no branch of the Service takes precedence over the other as regards ranks of officers; that is to say, a colonel of 1901, of say, a West Indian regiment, would precede a colonel of Guards, artillery or cavalry of 1902 promotion. Drawn up on a brigade parade, the cavalry take the right of the line; thus: artillery, Royal Engineers, footguards and regular regiments, garrison regiments and West Indian regiments, in the order named.

As regards Precedency between Officers of the combined Services a table of "Relative Rank and Precedency in the Army and Navy" should be consulted, as a post-captain in the navy after three years' service ranks with a colonel in the army, and a lieutenant or a navigating-lieutenant of eight years' standing ranks with a major in the army, and a lieutenant or a navigating-lieutenant in the navy of six years' standing ranks with a captain in the army, etc. Consulate officers also take precedence according to seniority of service in England and date of official arrival. The Foreign Office List of the current year should be consulted for date in each instance.

As regards the Precedence due to Widows bearing titles who have married again: The widow of a peer married to a commoner retains her title by courtesy, and the precedency due to the title is accorded to her.

The Widow of a Baronet married to a commoner retains her title by right and not by courtesy.

The Widow of a Knight married to a commoner retains her title by courtesy only, but the precedency due to the widow of a knight is accorded to her.

The Daughter of a Peer if married to a baronet or a commoner retains her precedency, but if married to a baron her precedency is merged in that of her husband.

When the Widow of a Duke marries a person of lower rank than that of her late husband, she still retains her precedency.

When the Daughter of a Duke marries a peer she takes the precedency due to the rank of her husband; if she marries a commoner, precedency is accorded to her due to the daughter of a duke.

Age confers no Precedency on either sex. Equals in rank from the highest to the lowest take precedence according to the creation of their title and not as regards the age of the person bearing the title. As, for instance, a youthful duke would take precedence of an aged duke, if the title of the youthful duke bore an earlier date than that of the aged duke. The same rule applies equally to baronets and knights.

When two earls are present at a dinner-party, the date of their respective patents of nobility decides the order of precedence due to them.

A host or hostess should always consult a " Peerage " or a " Baronetage " if in doubt as to the precedence due to expected guests bearing titles ; wealth or social position are not taken into account in this matter, it being strictly a question of date.

The Precedence due to Ladies of Equal Rank takes effect in the same manner. Thus, a young wife of a baronet takes precedence over the elderly wife of a baronet if the creation of her husband's title bears an earlier date.

When the Claims to Precedency of Persons of Equal Rank clash, the claims of a gentleman should be waived in favour of those of a lady, should the persons be of opposite sexes. Thus, if two couples of superior rank to the other guests were present at a dinner-party, the host should take down the lady of highest rank, and the hostess should be taken down by the gentleman of highest rank, in which case the lady second in rank should go in to dinner *before* her husband, although the gentleman taking her down to dinner were of lower rank than her husband.

Esquires, and the Wives of Esquires, take precedence according to their social position. Members of Parliament have no precedence, though it is often accorded to them as a matter of courtesy, especially in the county which they represent; the wives of members of Parliament are likewise entitled to no precedence on the ground of their husbands being members of Parliament.

The High Sheriff of a County takes precedence over all other gentlemen in the county, of whatever rank, save the lord-lieutenant, as a Royal warrant has been recently issued by His Majesty King Edward giving precedence to lord-lieutenants of counties before high sheriffs.

The High Sheriff out of his particular county has no precedence, neither has a lord-lieutenant; and the wives of either lords-lieutenants or high sheriffs take no precedence on account of their husbands' official dignity.

An Assize Judge takes precedence over the high sheriff as the assize judge represents the Sovereign of the Realm.

Clergymen, Barristers-at-Law, officers in the army and navy take precedence over esquires on account of such rank ; and in each profession precedence should be accorded them according to dignity, date of ordination, date of call, and date of commission in their several professions, assuming that the rank is equal.

High Clerical and Legal Dignitaries take special precedence; for instance, the Archbishop of Canterbury takes precedence of all dukes, and the Lord Chancellor takes precedence of the three archbishops—York, Armagh, and

Dublin—who also take precedence of dukes; bishops take precedence of all barons, whatever their date of creation. The Lord Chief Justice, the Master of the Rolls, when not peers, and all judges of the High Court of Justice in their various divisions, take precedence of baronets and of all knights, save the Knights of the Garter, who are beside the question.

The Relative Rank between Officers of the Army and Navy and doctors of divinity is somewhat difficult to determine as regards the precedence to be given them at a dinner-party. " Dod " places " esquires by office, which, of course, includes all officers of the army and navy," next *before* the younger sons of knights and before doctors in divinity, who follow next in order; while " Lodge " places " officers of the navy and army " *after* the younger sons of knights bachelor, clergymen, and barristers-at-law.

Precedency at Dinner-Parties.—When royalty is present at a dinner-party, a prince of blood royal takes precedence of a princess, and leads the way with the hostess, the host following next with the princess. On the other hand, a princess of the blood royal takes precedence of a foreign prince—her husband—and leads the way with the host.

The Host should take down the Lady of Highest Rank, and lead the way with her to the dining-room. The guests should follow the host in couples according to the degree of precedence due to them, and the hostess should follow the last couple with the gentleman of highest rank present.

When a Greater Number of Gentlemen than ladies are present at a dinner-party, as is often the case, these gentlemen should follow the hostess to the dining-room and not precede her.

When a Widow or Maiden Lady is Hostess, and there is no gentleman of the family present to act as host, the gentleman second in rank should take down the lady of highest rank, leading the way with her to the dining-room, the hostess following last, with the gentleman of highest rank.

In the Case of either a Husband's Sister or a wife's sister being required to act as hostess, precedence should be given to the wife's sister.

An Eldest Son's Wife should take precedence of her husband's sisters in his father's house.

As regards the precedence due to the relatives of a host or hostess, it should give way in favour of that due to the guests not related to the host or hostess, although their relatives might be, perhaps, of higher rank than the guests themselves.

Occasionally, the eldest son of the house acts as second host, taking down a lady second or third in rank; but the daughters of the house should always be taken down to dinner after the other ladies present, and in no case before them.

No precedence is accorded to either a lady or a gentleman by virtue of a mother's rank.

No precedence is accorded to brides in society, though occasionally in the country old-fashioned people consider it due to a bride to send her in to dinner with the host on the occasion of her first dining at a house within three months of her marriage.

Table of General Precedency

GENTLEMEN

The King.	The Sovereign's grandsons.
The Prince of Wales.	The Sovereign's brothers.
The Sovereign's younger sons.	The Sovereign's uncles.

The Sovereign's nephews.
Ambassadors.
Archbishop of Canterbury.
Lord High Chancellor.
Archbishop of York.
The Prime Minister.
Lord Chancellor of Ireland.
Lord President of the Council.
Lord Privy Seal.
Dukes who may happen to hold either of these five offices—
  1. Lord Great Chamberlain.
  2. Earl Marshal.
  3. Lord Steward.
  4. Lord Chamberlain.
  5. Master of the Horse.
Dukes in order of their patents of creation—
  1. Dukes of England.
  2. ,, Scotland.
  3. Dukes of Great Britain.
  4. ,, ,, Ireland created before the Union.
  5. Dukes created since the Union.
Eldest sons of Dukes of Blood Royal.
Marquesses who may hold either of the Offices of State named above.
Marquesses in same order as Dukes.
Dukes' eldest sons.
Earls holding either of the five Offices of State.
Earls in same order as Dukes.
Younger sons of Dukes of Blood Royal.
Marquesses' eldest sons.
Dukes' younger sons.
Viscounts who may hold either of the five Offices of State.
Viscounts in same order as Dukes.
Earls' eldest sons.
Marquesses' younger sons.
Bishop of London.
  ,, Durham.
  ,, Winchester.
Other English Bishops in order of their consecration.
Moderator of the Church of Scotland.

Barons holding either of the five Offices of State.
Barons who may be Secretaries of State or Irish Secretary.
Barons in same order as Dukes.
The Speaker of the House of Commons.
Treasurer of the Household.
Comptroller of the Household.
Vice-Chamberlain of the Household.
Secretaries of State below the rank of Barons.
Viscounts' eldest sons.
Earls' younger sons.
Barons' eldest sons.
Commoners who are Knights of the Garter.
Privy Councillors of rank lower than the foregoing, according to date they were sworn in.
Chancellor of the Exchequer.
  ,, ,, ,, Duchy of Lancaster.
Lord Chief Justice of England.
Master of the Rolls.
Lords Justices of Appeal and President of Probate Court.
Judges of the High Court of Justice.
Viscounts' younger sons.
Barons' ,, ,,
Sons of Life Peers.
Baronets according to dates of patents.
Knights Grand Cross of Bath.
Knights Grand Commanders, Star of India.
Knights Grand Cross of St. Michael and St. George.
Knights Grand Commanders of Indian Empire.
Knights Grand Cross of Royal Victorian Order.
Knights Commanders of above Orders in same sequence.
Knights Bachelors of above Orders in same sequence.
Commanders of the Royal Victorian Order.
Judges of County Courts in

England and Ireland, and Judges of the City of London Court.

Serjeants-at-Law.

Masters in Lunacy.

Companions of Orders of Bath, Star of India, SS. Michael and George, and Indian Empire in same sequence.

Members of 4th class of Royal Victorian Order.

Companions of Distinguished Service Order.

Eldest sons of younger sons of Peers.

Baronets' eldest sons.

Knights' eldest sons, in order of their fathers.

Members of 5th class of Royal Victorian Order.

Younger sons of Peers' younger sons.

Baronets' younger sons.

Knights' younger sons, in order of their fathers.

Naval, Military, and other Esquires by Office.

Gentlemen entitled to bear Coat Armour.

LADIES

The Queen.

The Queen Mother.

The Sovereign's daughters.

Wives of Sovereign's younger sons.

Sovereign's granddaughters.

Wives of Sovereign's grandsons.

Sovereign's sisters.

Wives of Sovereign's brothers.

Sovereign's aunts.

Wives of Sovereign's uncles.

Sovereign's nieces.

Wives of Sovereign's nephews.

Duchesses (in same order as Dukes).

Wives of eldest sons of Dukes of Blood Royal.

Marchionesses.

Wives of eldest sons of Dukes.

Daughters of Dukes.

Countesses.

Wives of younger sons of Royal Dukes.

Wives of eldest sons of Marquesses.

Daughters of Marquesses.

Wives of younger sons of Dukes.

Viscountesses.

Wives of eldest sons of Earls.

Daughters of Earls.

Wives of younger sons of Marquesses.

Baronesses.

Wives of eldest sons of Viscounts.

Daughters of Viscounts.

Wives of younger sons of Earls.

Wives of eldest sons of Barons.

Daughters of Barons.

Maids of Honour.

Wives of younger sons of Viscounts.

Wives of younger sons of Barons.

Daughters and sons' wives of Life Peers.

Wives of Baronets.

Daughters of Baronets.

Wives of eldest sons of Knights.

Daughters of Knights.

Wives of younger sons of Peers' younger sons.

Wives of younger sons of Baronets.

Wives of younger sons of Knights.

Wives of Esquires.

Wives of Gentlemen.

CHAPTER VI

THE colloquial application of titles differs materially from the application of titles when not used colloquially, and many persons are in doubt as to whether they should or should not make use colloquially of titles in full.

His Majesty the King should be addressed as " Sir " by all those who come in social contact with him ; and by all others as " Your Majesty."

Her Majesty Queen Mary should be addressed as " Ma'm " by all those who come in social contact with her ; and by all others as " Your Majesty."

Her Majesty Queen Alexandra should be addressed as " Ma'm " by all those who come in social contact with her ; and by all others as " Your Majesty."

The Prince of Wales, the Duke of Connaught, and all princes of the blood royal, should be addressed by the upper classes as " Sir."

The princesses of the blood royal, should be addressed as " Ma'm " by the upper classes. The wives of the princes of the blood royal should also be addressed as " Ma'm " by the upper classes.

The German Emperor should be addressed as " Sir " by the upper classes.

The King of Spain should be addressed as " Sir " by the upper classes ; the Queen of Spain should be addressed as " Ma'm " by the upper classes.

A foreign prince bearing the title of serene highness should be addressed as " Prince," and not as " Sir," by the

E

aristocracy and gentry, and as " Your Serene Highness " by all other classes.

A foreign princess, also bearing the title of serene highness, should be styled "Princess" when addressed colloquially by the upper classes, but not as " Ma'am "; and as " Your Serene Highness " by all other classes.

An English duke should be addressed as " Duke " by the aristocracy and gentry, and not as " Your Grace " by members of either of these classes. All other classes should address him colloquially as "Your Grace."

An English duchess should be addressed as " Duchess " by all persons conversing with her belonging to the upper classes, and as " Your Grace " by all other classes.

A marquess, colloquially, should be addressed as " Lord A."

A marchioness should be addressed as "Lady A." by the upper classes. It would be a mistake to address an English marquess as " Marquess," or a marchioness as " Marchioness," colloquially speaking. All other classes should address them either as " My Lord " or " Your Lordship," " My Lady " or " Your Ladyship."

An earl should be addressed as " Lord B." by the upper classes, and as " My Lord " or " Your Lordship " by all other classes.

A countess should be addressed as " Lady B." by the upper classes, and as " My Lady " or " Your Ladyship " by all other classes.

A viscount should be addressed as " Lord C." by the upper classes, and as " My Lord " or " Your Lordship " by all other classes.

A viscountess should be addressed as " Lady C." by the upper classes, and as " My Lady " or " Your Ladyship " by all other classes.

A baron should be addressed as " Lord D." by the upper classes, and as " My Lord " or " Your Lordship " by all other classes.

A baroness should be addressed as " Lady D." by the upper classes, and as " My Lady " or " Your Ladyship " by all other classes.

In strictly official or business intercourse a marquess, an earl, a viscount, a baron, and a younger son of a duke or marquis, should be addressed as " My Lord."

The eldest son of a duke should be addressed as " Lord A." by the upper classes, and as " My Lord " or " Your Lordship " by all other classes.

The wife of the eldest son of a duke should be addressed as " Lady A." by the upper classes, and as " My Lady " or " Your Ladyship " by all other classes.

The younger sons of a duke should be addressed as " Lord John E." or " Lord Charles E." by the upper classes, and as " My Lord " or " Your Lordship " by all other classes. Persons well acquainted with them would address them colloquially by their title and christian name, as "Lord John" or "Lord Charles." The same remark applies to their wives, who are often colloquially addressed as " Lady Alfred " or " Lady Edward."

The wives of the younger sons of a duke should be addressed as " Lady John E." or " Lady Charles E." by the upper classes, and as " My Lady " or " Your Ladyship " by all other classes.

The daughters of a duke should be addressed as " Lady Mary A." or " Lady Elizabeth B." by the upper classes, and as " Lady Mary " and " Lady Elizabeth " by those intimate with them, and as " My Lady " or " Your Ladyship " by all other classes.

The eldest son of a marquess should be addressed as " Lord A." by the upper classes, and as " My Lord " or " Your Lordship " by all other classes.

The wife of the eldest son of a marquis should be addressed as " Lady A." by the upper classes, and as " My Lady " or " Your Ladyship " by all other classes.

The younger sons of a marquis should be addressed as

"Lord Henry B." and "Lord Frederick B." by the upper classes, and as "My Lord" or "Your Lordship" by all other classes.

The wives of the younger sons of a marquis should be addressed as "Lady Henry B." and "Lady Frederick B." by the upper classes, and as "My Lady" or "Your Ladyship" by all other classes.

The daughters of a marquis should be addressed as "Lady Florence B." and "Lady Sarah B." by the upper classes, and as "My Lady" or "Your Ladyship" by all other classes.

The eldest son of an earl should be addressed as "Lord C." by the upper classes, and as "My Lord" or "Your Lordship" by all other classes.

The wife of the eldest son of an earl should be addressed as "Lady C." by the upper classes, and as "My Lady" or "Your Ladyship" by all other classes.

The daughters of an earl should be addressed as "Lady Blanche" and "Lady Evelyn" by the upper classes, and as "My Lady" or "Your Ladyship" by all other classes.

The younger sons of earls, and both eldest and younger sons of viscounts and barons, only bear the courtesy title of honourable. The daughters of viscounts aud barons also bear the courtesy title of honourable. But this title of honourable should never be used colloquially under any circumstances. The Honourable Mr. or Mrs. B., or the Honourable Miss B., should be styled Mr., Mrs., or Miss B.

Baronets should be addressed by their full title and surname, as Sir John Blank, by the upper classes, and by their titles and christian names only by all other classes.

Baronets' wives should be addressed as "Lady B." or "Lady C.," according to the surnames of their husbands: thus, "Sir John Blank's" wife should be addressed as "Lady Blank" by the upper classes, not as "Lady John Blank"—to do so would be to give her the rank of the wife of the younger son of a duke or marquis instead of that of a baronet's wife only—and as "My Lady" or "Your Ladyship" by all other classes.

The wives of knights should be addressed as "Lady B." or "Lady C.," according to the surnames of their husbands : thus, "Sir John Blank's" wife should be addressed as "Lady Blank" by the upper classes, and as "My Lady" or "Your Ladyship" by all other classes.

In addressing Foreigners of Rank colloquially, the received rule is to address them by their individual titles and surnames.

A prince or princess should be addressed by their full title : thus, "Prince Munich," or "Princess Munich," by the upper classes. Persons intimate with them usually address them as "Prince" or "Princess," as the case may be.

In the case of a prince being a younger son, and not the reigning head of the house, his christian name is generally used after his title when addressing him : thus, "Prince Louis," in lieu of "Prince" only. The same remark applies to the unmarried daughters of princes. They also should be addressed by their christian name, in addition to their title of "Princess," by the aristocracy and gentry, and as "Your Serene" or "Your Imperial Highness," according to their birth and title, by all other classes.

A French duke should be addressed by his surname, with the addition of monsieur : thus, "Monsieur de Rouen," by the upper classes, and as "Monsieur le Duc" by all other classes.

A French duchess should be addressed by her surname, with the addition of madame : thus, "Madame de Rouen" by the upper classes, and as "Madame la Duchesse" by all other classes.

A marquis should be addressed by his surname, with the addition of monsieur : thus, "Monsieur de Harfleur" by the upper classes, and as "Monsieur le Marquis" by all other classes.

A marquise should be addressed by her surname, with the addition of madame: thus, " Madame la Harfleur" by the upper classes, and as " Madame la Marquise " by all other classes.

A comte should be addressed by his surname, with the addition of monsieur : thus, " Monsieur de Montpellier" by the upper classes, and as " Monsieur le Comte" by all other classes.

A comtesse should be addressed by her surname, with the addition of madame : thus, " Madame de Montpellier" by the upper classes, and as " Madame la Comtesse " by all other classes.

A vicomte should be addressed by his surname, with the addition of monsieur : thus, " Monsieur de Toulouse " by the upper classes, and as " Monsieur le Vicomte " by all other classes.

A vicomtesse should be addressed by her surname, with the addition of madame : thus, " Madame de Toulouse " by the upper classes, and as " Madame la Vicomtesse " by all other classes.

A baron should be addressed by his surname, with the addition of monsieur : thus, " Monsieur d'Avignon " by the upper classes, and as " Monsieur le Baron" by all other classes.

A baronne should be addressed by her surname, with the addition of madame : thus, " Madame d'Avignon" by the upper classes, and as " Madame la Baronne" by all other classes.

A young unmarried lady should be addressed as " Mademoiselle d'Avignon" by the upper classes, and as " Mademoiselle" by all other classes.

In German titles the distinction of " Von " before the surname is seldom used colloquially, the title and surname being used without the prefix of " Von." Thus, " Count von Ausberg " should be addressed as " Count Ausberg " in conversation, and not as " Monsieur le Comte."

Foreign ladies of rank should, when German or Russian, etc., be addressed by their title and surname, and not by their title only, and the prefix "Von" should be omitted; but in the case of a French or Italian title the "de" or "de la" before the surname 'should on no account be omitted.

When Englishmen are extremely intimate with foreigners of rank they would, in conversation, probably address them by their surnames; but only thorough intimacy and friendship warrants this familiarity.

As regards addressing the Clergy, an archbishop should be addressed 'colloquially as "Your Grace" or "Archbishop" by the upper classes, and as "Your Grace" by the clergy and all other classes.

A bishop should be addressed colloquially as "My Lord" or "Bishop of Dash" or "Bishop" by the upper classes, and as "My Lord" by the clergy and all other classes.

A dean should be styled "Mr. Dean," "Dean Dash," or "Dean," by the upper classes.

An archdeacon should be addressed as "Archdeacon Dash," and a canon as "Canon Dash."

The wives of archbishops, bishops, and deans 'should be respectively addressed as "Mrs. A.," "Mrs. B.," or "Mrs. C." They take no title from the spiritual rank of their husbands.

Officers in the Army should be respectively addressed as "General A.," "Colonel B.," "Major C.," or "Captain D.," and not as "General," "Colonel," or "Major," except by their very intimate friends.

The wives of officers should be addressed as "Mrs. A.," "Mrs. B.," "Mrs. C.," or "Mrs. D." They should never be addressed as "Mrs. General A.," "Mrs. Colonel B.," "Mrs. Major C.," or "Mrs. Captain D."

A lady should not address her husband colloquially by his surname only, as "Jones," "Brown," or by whatever his surname might be, or speak of him without the prefix of "Mr."

The usual rule is for a wife to speak of her husband as "Mr. Brown," or "My husband," except to intimate friends, when the christian name only is frequently used, and to address him by his christian name only.

A wife should not address her husband by the initial letter of his surname, as "Mr. B." or "Mr. P."; neither should a husband address his wife by the initial letter of his surname.

When intimate friends address each other by the initial letter of their names it is by way of pleasantry only, and such cases, of course, do not come within the rules of etiquette.

Peeresses frequently address their husbands, and speak of them, by the name attached to their title, in place of using their christian or family name. Thus, the "Earl of Blankshire" would be styled "Blankshire" by his wife, without the prefix of "Lord," and his usual signature would be "Blankshire," without the addition of any christian name.

Baronets' wives should not address their husbands by their surnames, but by their christian names, and should speak of them as "Sir George" or "Sir John."

The wives of knights also should not address their husbands by their surnames, but by their christian names. and should speak of them as "Sir George" or "Sir John."

The Lord Mayor should be addressed as "Lord Mayor," colloquially, and the Lady Mayoress as "Lady Mayoress," unless the Lord Mayor during office is created a baronet or receives the honour of knighthood, when he should be addressed as "Sir John" or "Sir Henry," and his wife as "Lady A."

CHAPTER VII

GENERAL society is now very frequently brought into contact with royalty—members of the Royal Family of England and members of various royal families of Europe.

With His Majesty this association is of frequent occurrence as regards the general public, and persons possessing special interest are constantly brought into communication with him.

Strict Court etiquette is greatly in abeyance, and laid aside by His Majesty when paying visits to personal friends, or when receiving visits from the same.

The geniality of the English princes and princesses is everywhere acknowledged, and the restrictions of Court etiquette are frequently relaxed by their desire when visiting at the houses of the nobility and gentry.

The etiquette that reigns in foreign Courts—Austria, Russia, Greece, etc.—is seldom waived, and is adhered to with much punctilio. So much so is this the case with certain foreign princes who visit our shores, that the observances they claim as due to their exalted position are often felt to be a restraint upon the hosts whom they honour with their company, in town or country, at dinner, ball, or country-house party.

On the other hand, many royal personages who occasionally visit England are unbending and unceremonious towards society in general.

When royal personages visit London for a few weeks,

whether located at palace, embassy, or hotel, it is etiquette for any person who is personally acquainted with or connected in any way with their Court or cabinet, or who has been presented at their Court, to leave cards on them and write their names in their visiting books. Persons still higher in the social scale, give receptions in their honour, and invite them to stay at their princely mansions.

When such visits are paid, the principal neighbours are usually invited to meet the royal guests at dinner, ball, or reception, and on the invitation card is written, "To meet H.R.H. the Crown Prince of ——," or "Her Serene Highness the Grand Duchess of ——," etc.; but a hostess exercises her own discretion respecting the invitations she issues.

If a ball is in contemplation the county at large is invited to the mansion, but if dinner invitations only are issued, then the circle is necessarily restricted to a favoured few.

The neighbours who are not invited to a house where a royal guest is staying should avoid calling on the hostess until the departure of the royal visitors, even if calls are due.

The principal people of a county who happen to be present at an entertainment, either dinner or dance, are usually presented to the royal guests by the host or hostess, permission to do so having been first solicited.

When the person to be presented is a person of rank or distinction, it would only be necessary to say, "May I present Lord A., or General B., to you, Sir?" but if the person to be presented has no particular claim to the honour beyond being popular in the county, the request should be prefaced with a few words of explanation respecting the person to be presented.

When the name or fame of those presented has reached the ears of the royal guests, they usually shake hands on the presentation being made, and enter into conversation with them; otherwise they merely bow, and make one or two passing remarks.

A house-party is generally composed of those with whom a royal guest is more or less acquainted. When the party includes any one who is a stranger to the royal guests, he or she should be presented on the first opportunity.

The members of the Royal Family have each, more or less, their particular set, as have also the foreign princes who periodically visit this country, and therefore house-parties are usually made up of those moving in the set of the expected prince.

For the proper mode of addressing royal personages, see Chapter VI.

As regards royal invitations, all invitations from the Sovereign are commands, and must be answered and obeyed as such, and the word " command " must be made use of in answering such invitations. If any reason exists for not obeying His Majesty's commands it should be stated.

Invitations from members of the Royal Family are treated by courtesy as commands, but in replying to such invitations the word " command " should not be used. The answers to such invitations should be addressed to the Comptroller of the Household, by whom they are usually issued.

Answers to royal invitations should be written in the third person, and reasons given for non-acceptance.

A previous engagement cannot be pleaded as an excuse for refusing a royal invitation; only personal indisposition or serious illness, or death of near relatives, would be adequate reasons for not accepting a royal invitation.

When a royal invitation is verbally given, the answer should be verbal also.

At all entertainments at which royal guests are present they should be received by the host and hostess in the entrance-hall. In the case of serene highnesses they should be received by the host and conducted by him to the hostess ; this rule equally applies to the reception of eastern princes.

The etiquette to be observed on the departure of royal personages is identical with that observed on their arrival.

With regard to inviting members of the Royal Family to assist at the opening of any public undertaking, the request should be made through the Comptroller of the Household of the prince who is to be invited, or through his secretary, and the same rule equally applies to both prince and princess.

Indian Princes.—The exact status of Indian princes has never been actually laid down, but all who are " Highnesses " are given precedence at the English Court and in society after the Royal Family and foreign princes. In the procession at Court entertainments they go in front of ambassadors.

No Indian prince is considered to be of blood royal, and they do not stand in the line at levées and Courts, but all have the private *Entrée.*

CHAPTER VIII

THE acquaintanceship of foreign residents is of considerable service to English people purposing to winter abroad, or to remain for any length of time in a continental city, as by its means they obtain an entrance into foreign society. An introduction to the English Ambassador or Minister at a foreign Court is of still greater service in this matter.

People of recognised position in society have the privilege of leaving cards at the English Embassy at any foreign city in which they intend making a temporary stay.

So thoroughly is the position of English travellers known to the English Ministry at a foreign Court, that should a person, who is not received in English society, leave cards at the English Embassy, they would be at once returned as an intimation that the acquaintance is declined.

It is erroneous to suppose that by leaving cards upon foreigners of distinction, an acquaintanceship can be commenced, for unless introductions have been formally made, leaving cards is a useless proceeding.

At far-away spots little frequented by the general run of travellers, and where there are but few, if any, resident English, travellers requiring advice or assistance from the English consul, can, without an introduction, call upon him, nationality being the ground upon which to do this, and if of equal social standing, they would be received with social consideration; if otherwise, all assistance would be given to them from an official point of view. Many people when travelling abroad make pleasant acquaintances even without the help of introductions, the occasion of a meeting being as it were a semi-introduction in itself.

Such casual acquaintanceships are, however, attended with certain risks, especially to persons who have been absent from England some little time, or who when in England have entered comparatively but little in society, and who are thus apt to drift unawares into close friendships with people perhaps well bred and agreeable, although tabooed at home for some good and sufficient reason. *Contretemps* such as these are painful to kind-hearted people when subsequently compelled to avoid and to relinquish the acquaintance of those with whom they have become pleasantly intimate. An introduction to an English resident in either town or city obviates any unpleasantness of this nature, as one so situated is generally kept *au courant* with all that takes place in society at home.

When persons desire to enter into society abroad they endeavour to obtain letters of introduction from friends and acquaintances to residents in the cities they purpose visiting.

Unless English travellers have been duly presented at the Court of St. James's, they cannot obtain presentations at foreign Courts through the English Embassies.

When a lady desires a presentation at a foreign Court, she should write to the English Ambassadress and request the honour of a presentation, and should state the date of her presentation and the name of the lady by whom she was presented. After her statement has been duly verified the request is granted. In a like manner when a gentleman desires a presentation at a foreign Court, he should write to the Ambassador and request the honour of a presentation, and should state the date of the Levée at which he was presented, and the name of the person by whom the presentation was made.

Presentations at foreign Courts take place in the evening, and the persons to be presented, and those who attend, assemble previous to the entrance of the royal personages: the rule is for the grand *maitresse* to present each lady in turn to her royal mistress, who makes the tour of the apartment for this purpose, and addresses some courteous observation to each.

CHAPTER IX

THERE are, perhaps, two reasons why various surnames are so frequently mispronounced, the one being unfamiliarity with the freak of fashion which governs the pronunciation of certain well-known names, the other ignorance, or want of education.

When sensitive persons hear a name pronounced differently from the way in which they have themselves but just pronounced it, and in a tone and manner strongly suggestive of correction, it is wounding to their *amour propre*.

As a rule, when persons are in doubt as to the correct pronunciation of any particular name, it would be best to avoid mentioning it, if possible, until their doubts are set at rest by some one better informed than themselves.

Names that have a fashionable or peculiar pronunciation, or are pronounced otherwise than as they are spelt, are but few, and names which it is possible wrongly to accent are also not very numerous ; but it is surprising how often these names occur in the course of conversation.

The names of distinguished artists that are open to mispronunciation occur far oftener in conversation than do the general run of uncommon surnames.

There are many celebrated hunts and hunting quarters of which the names are open to considerable mispronunciation.

With regard to placing the accent on the wrong syllable in the pronunciation of names, it requires but little thought to avoid making this mistake, a popular error being that of placing the accent upon the last syllable of a name; whereas, in a name of two syllables, the accent should invariably be placed upon the first, and the second syllable should be as it were slightly abbreviated or slightly altered.

In names of three syllables the error usually consists in placing the accent upon the last syllable, whereas the accent should be placed upon the second syllable. There are occasional exceptions to this rule, and the few names given in this chapter, both as regards their pronunciation and accentuation, will serve as a useful guide in the pronunciation of uncommon names.

SPELT.	PRONOUNCED.	REMARKS.
Abergavenny.	Abergen'ny.	*Av* not sounded.
Arbuthnot.	Arbuth'not.	
Arundel.	Arrandel.	
Beaconsfield.	Beckonsfield.	
Beauchamp.	Bea'cham.	
Beauclerk or } Beauclerc. }	Bo'clair.	Accent on first syllable.
Belvoir.	Be'ver.	
Berkely.	Bark'ley.	
Bethune.	Bee'ton.	
Bicester.	Bis'ter.	Accent on first syllable.
Blount.	Blunt.	
Blyth.	Bly.	*Th* not sounded.
Bourke.	Burk.	
Bourne.	Burn.	
Bowles.	Boles.	
Breadalbane.	Breaddal'bane.	Accent on second syllable.
Brougham.	Broum.	
Buchan.	Buck'an.	Accent on first syllable.
Burdett.	Burdett'.	Accent on last syllable.
Burnett.	Burnett'.	Accent on last syllable.
Bury.	Berry.	
Calderon.	Cal'dron not Cauldron.	
Charteris.	Charters.	
Cholmeley.	Chum'ley.	
Cholmondeley.	,,	
Cirencester.	Cis'ester.	Accent on first syllable.
Clanricarde.	Clanrecarde.	Accent on second sylla- ble.

F

SPELT.	PRONOUNCED.	REMARKS.
Cockburn.	Cōburn.	*Ck* not sounded.
Colquhoun.	Koohoon'.	Accent on last syllable.
Conynham.	Cunyingham.	
Coutts.	Koots.	
Cowper.	Couper.	
Dalziel.	Dee'al.	Accent on first syllable.
Derby.	Darby.	
Des Vaux.	Deveu.	The *x* not sounded.
Devereux.	Devereu.	The *x* not sounded.
Dillwyn.	Dil'lun.	The *wy* takes the sound of *u ;* the accent on first syllable.
Duchesne.	Dukarn.	
Du Plat.	Du Plar.	
Elgin.		The *g* hard as in give.
Eyre.	Air.	
Fildes.	Filedes.	Not Filldes.
Fortescue.	Fort'iskew.	
Geoffrey.	Jefrey.	
Geoghegan.	Gaygan.	
Gifford.	Jifford.	The *g* soft as in George.
Gillett.		*G* hard as in Gilbert.
Gillott.		*G* hard.
Glamis.	Glarms.	
Gorges.	Gor'jes.	First *g* hard and second *g* soft.
Gough.	Goff.	
Gower.	Gor.	But Gower as regards the street of that name with the general public.
Harcourt.	Har'kut.	Accent on first syllable.
Heathcote.	Heth'kut.	
Hertford.	Har'ford.	
Home.	Hume.	
Hughes.	Hews.	
Jervis.	Jarvis.	
Johnstone.		The *t* not sounded.
Kennaird.	Kennaird'.	Accent on last syllable.
Kennard.	Kennard'.	Accent on last syllable.
Ker.	Kar.	
Knollys.	Knowls.	
Layard.	Laird.	
Leconfield.	Lek'onfield.	

SPELT.	PRONOUNCED.	REMARKS.
Lefevre.	Lefavre.	
Leigh.	Lee.	
Lyvedon.	Livden.	
Macnamara.	Macnemar'ar.	Accent on third syllable.
Mainwaring.	Man'nering.	
Marjoribanks.	Marshbanks.	
McIntosh.	Makintosh.	
McLeod.	McCloud.	
Menzies.	Myng'es.	Accent on first syllable.
Meux.	Mews.	The *x* sounded as *s*.
Millais.	Mil'lay.	Accent on first syllable.
Milnes.	Mills.	
Molyneux.		The *x* sounded, with slight accent on last syllable.
Monck.	Munk.	
Monckton.	Munk'ton.	Accent on first syllable.
Monson.	Munson.	
Montgomerie or Montgomery.	Mungum'ery.	Accent on second syllable.
Mowbray.	Mobrey.	
Nigel.	Ni'jel.	
Ouless.	Ooless.	
Parnell.	Parnell'.	Accent on last syllable.
Pepys.	Pep'is.	Accent on first syllable.
Pierrepont.	Pierpont.	
Ponsonby.	Punsonby.	
Pontefract.	Pomfret.	
Pugh.	Pew.	
Pytchley.	Pȳtch'ley.	Not Pitchley.
Ruthven.	Riv'en.	
Sandys.	Sands.	
St. Clair.	Sinclair.	
St. Maur.	See'mor, or S'nt Maur.	
St. John.	Sinjin.	As regards christian and surname, but as St. John when applied to church or locality.
Seymour.	Sey'mer.	Accent on first syllable.
Strachan.	Strawn.	
Tadema.	Tad'ymar.	Accent on first syllable.
Tollemache.	Tollmash.	

SPELT.	PRONOUNCED.	REMARKS.
Trafalgar.	Trafalgar'.	Accent on last syllable ; as regards the peer of that name, not otherwise.
Tredegar.	Trede'gar.	Accent on second syllable.
Tremayne.	Tremayne'.	Accent on last syllable.
Tyrrwhitt.	Tirritt.	
Vaughan.	Vorn.	
Vaux.		The *x* sounded.
Villbois.	Vealbwor.	
Villiers.	Vil'lers.	
Waldegrave.	Wal'grave.	The *de* not sounded.
Wemyss.	Weems.	
Willoughby D'Eresby.	Willowby D'Ersby.	

CHAPTER X

Courts are now held in lieu of Drawing-rooms by Their Majesties the King and Queen at Buckingham Palace, and at which Presentations to Their Majesties are made.

These Courts are held in the evenings at ten o'clock, but the hour at which the company should commence to arrive is intimated by the Lord Chamberlain in the notice issued of the Courts to be held.

Two Courts are usually, but not invariably, held before Easter, and two more after Easter.

Ladies who have been presented at Drawing-rooms and Courts, held during the last two reigns, do not require to be again presented to Their Majesties the King and Queen; thus, ladies who have already been presented at these Drawing-rooms, and who are desirous of being invited to one or other of these Courts, and who are also desirous of making presentations, should send in their names and the names of those to be presented by them to the Lord Chamberlain, St. James's Palace, S.W., on, or as soon as possible after, the 1st of January in each year, but not before that month.

Ladies are also privileged to mention at the same time when it will be most convenient to them to pay their respects to Their Majesties. If it should not be convenient for a lady to attend or be presented at the particular Court to which she is invited, it will be open to her to make her excuses to the Lord Chamberlain in writing, when her name can, if desired, and if possible, be transferred to another list.

A lady who makes a presentation to Their Majesties, must be personally acquainted with and responsible for the lady she presents. She must herself attend the Court, and cannot present more than one lady in addition to her daughters or daughters-in-law. The numbers received at each Court being necessarily limited, ladies can only receive occasional invitations. Therefore, those who cannot be included in the year's list of invitations will receive an intimation to this effect from the Lord Chamberlain in answer to their applications to attend.

The Persons entitled to be presented at Their Majesties' Courts are the wives and daughters of the members of the aristocracy, the wives and daughters of those holding high official appointments in the Government, the wives and daughters of Members of Parliament, the county gentry and town gentry, the wives and daughters of the members of the legal, military, naval, clerical, medical, and other professions, the wives and daughters of merchants, bankers, and members of the Stock Exchange, and persons engaged in commerce on a large scale.

Although the word " gentry " is thus elastic, and although persons coming within the category might be fairly entitled to the privilege of attending Courts, yet it is well understood that birth, wealth, associations, and position give a *raison d'être* for such privilege ; as, for instance, the wife and daughters of an officer in the navy or a line regiment, whose means are slender, and whose position is obscure, would not be justified for these reasons in attending a Court, although the officer himself might attend a levée if desirous of doing so ; and this remark equally applies to the wives and daughters of clergymen, barristers, and others similarly situated.

Presentations to Their Majesties are made officially by the various foreign ambassadresses, by the wives of the members of the Cabinet, and by the wives of other official personages in various departments of the State, either civil, military, naval, or clerical.

Presentations at each of Their Majesties' Courts are now limited by royal command.

Presentations to Their Majesties should be made either by a relative or a friend of the lady presented who has herself been previously presented.

A lady has the privilege of presenting one lady only at a Court in addition to her daughters or daughters-in-law.

This restriction does not apply to ladies who, from official position or other circumstances, are specially privileged to make presentations to Their Majesties.

When a presentation is not made officially or by a near relative it is considered a favour on the part of the person making the presentation towards the person presented.

The responsibility of a presentation rests upon the person who makes it, both as to the social and moral fitness of the person presented; therefore, to solicit the favour of a presentation from a friend is to incur a considerable obligation, and it is a favour ladies have no hesitation in refusing unless good reasons exist for granting it.

When presentations are made through official channels the responsibility rests upon the " office " rather than upon the person making the presentation; hence presentations so made have little personal significance to the person making them.

A Lady having been presented on her Marriage has the privilege of attending, by invitation, any subsequent Court, but ladies who have no official position will only be allowed to attend a Court by summons every third year. On the accession of her husband to any title, she would again have to be presented, and should she marry a second time another presentation would be necessary to entitle her to attend one of Their Majesties' Courts.

It is the Privilege of the Married Lady to make Presentations, but should any person be presented whose antecedents or present position renders her socially unqualified to be presented, the Lord Chamberlain, on becoming aware of the fact, would at once cancel the presentation, and officially announce it in the *Gazette*, and the person making such presentation would be expected to tender an apology for so doing.

An Unmarried Lady does not possess the Privilege of making a presentation, however high her rank may be. She is not permitted to attend any subsequent Courts after first presentation until three years have elapsed; save under exceptional circumstances.

Four Courts are held during each year at Buckingham Palace, two before and two after Easter, but due intimation is given previous to each Court being held by the Lord Chamberlain through the medium of the official *Gazette*, from whence it is copied into the newspapers.

The wives of members of the Cabinet and of the ambassadors or ministers at the Court of St. James's usually attend at each Court, and have the privilege of doing so by reason of the official presentations made by them at each Court.

It is compulsory for a Lady making a presentation to be herself present at the Court at which the presentation is to be made, though it is not necessary for her to accompany the person whom she presents, but simply to attend the same Court.

When a Lady intends making a Presentation she should, on or after the 1st of January write to the Lord

Chamberlain and inform him of a wish to attend a Court, and forward the name of the lady to be presented by her.

Ladies are not expected to attend Court more than once in every three years, unless under exceptional circumstances.

A Lady attending a Court may present one lady in addition to her daughter or daughter-in-law.

A Lady presented for the First Time can only present her daughter or daughter-in-law at the Court at which she is presented.

No Applications can be received from ladies who wish to be presented. Their names must be forwarded by the ladies who wish to make the presentations.

Summonses are issued about three weeks before the date of each Court.

Ladies may be accompanied to Court by their husbands if the latter have been presented, but gentlemen do not pass before the King and Queen. Ladies are requested to forward the names of their husbands at the same time as their own, in order that they may be submitted together, as once the summons has been issued the amending of a summons card in order to include a lady's husband can only be permitted under the most exceptional circumstances.

Those who have the Privilege of the Entrée enter at the gate of the Palace situated outside Buckingham Gate. Those who possess this privilege are the diplomatic circle, the Cabinet ministers and their wives, and the members of the Household. The rooms, two in number, next to the Presence Chamber, are appropriated to them. All who have the privilege of the *entrée* are received by Their Majesties before the general circle, and according to their individual precedency, and they have also the privilege of making the first presentations.

When a Lady arrives at the Palace she should leave her wraps in the cloak-room with one of the maids in attendance. After crossing the Great Hall, she then makes her way up the Grand Staircase to the Corridor, where she shows her invitation-card to the page-in-waiting, and then passes on to one of the saloons.

When a lady arrives early she gains admission to the saloon next to those reserved for the *entrée*. When she arrives late she has to take her place in a further room of the suite according to the number of persons present.

The gentlemen-at-arms stationed at the door of each room close the gilt barriers when they consider the saloons are full. Chairs and benches are placed in the corridor and in these saloons for the accommodation of ladies thus waiting their turn to enter the Throne-room or Presence Chamber.

As the ladies quit each room for the Presence Chamber, others take their places, and the barriers are again closed, and this is continued until every one has been received.

A lady has to pass through the two *entrée* saloons before reaching the Picture Gallery.

At the door of the Picture Gallery a lady's train, which she has hitherto carried on her arm, is let down by two officials in attendance, and spread out by them with their wands ; she should cross the gallery with her train down to the Presence Chamber, at the door of which she should give the card of invitation she has brought with her to the official stationed there to receive it.

A Lady on being presented, curtsys to the King and curtsys to the Queen. The King bows in return, as does also the Queen. A lady presented does not kiss the Queen's hand, as she formerly did. The King does not shake hands with any present, however high their rank may be, neither does the Queen shake hands with any present.

A lady on being presented does not now curtsy to any

member of the Royal Family when she has passed Their
Majesties, and leaves the Presence Chamber, stepping
backwards, facing the royal party, until making her exit from
the apartment, when an official places her train on her arm
at the threshold of the doorway.

When a Lady wishes to attend a Court, after
having been duly presented, it is necessary to inform the
Lord Chamberlain of her wish to attend. Summonses are
issued about three weeks before the date of each Court.

Having received a summons to attend a Court she
should take the summons card with her, which she should
show to the page-in-waiting in the corridor, and eventually
hand it to the official stationed at the door of the Presence
Chamber, by whom it is passed on to the Lord Chamberlain,
who announces the name to Their Majesties.

A lady attending a Court curtsys to the King; she also
curtsys to the Queen, but does not curtsy to any other
member of the Royal Family present.

In the General Circle there is no Precedency
as to the order in which ladies attending a Court enter the
Presence Chamber. The earliest arrivals are the first to
appear before Their Majesties, without reference to rank
or position; and the same rule applies to ladies who are
presented, or to ladies who make presentations.

A Married Lady presented at a Court can, at the
same Court, present her daughter or daughter-in-law; but
in this case the one presented by her should enter the
Presence Chamber after her, and not before her.

Although, according to present regulations, the unmarried
daughters of members of the nobility and gentry who have
already been presented are only expected to attend a Court
once in every three years, it will not prevent their being

invited to Court functions, to the State balls, concerts, and garden parties.

Ladies who have been presented at a Court have the privilege of writing their names in Their Majesties' visiting book at Buckingham Palace once during the season. The hours of calling for this purpose are generally from three to five o'clock in the afternoon.

It is Imperative for Ladies to wear Full Court Dress when attending or being presented at a Court, viz. low bodice, short sleeves, and train to dress not less than three yards and a half in length.

Whether the train is cut round or square, or fastened from the shoulders or from beneath the bodice, is a matter of inclination or fashion.

It is also imperative that a presentation-dress should be white, if the person presented be an unmarried lady; and it is also the fashion for married ladies to wear white on their presentation, unless their age renders their doing so unsuitable.

The white dresses worn by either *débutantes* or married ladies may be trimmed with either coloured or white flowers, according to individual taste.

High Court Dress.—The Queen has been pleased to permit that a high Court dress of silk, satin, or velvet, may be worn at Their Majesties' Courts, and on other State occasions, by ladies, to whom, from illness, infirmity, or advancing age, the present low Court dress is inappropriate, viz.: Bodices in front, cut square, or heart-shaped, which may be filled in with white only, either transparent or lined; at the back, high, or cut down three-quarters height. Sleeves to elbow, either thick or transparent.

Trains, gloves, and feathers as usual.

It is necessary for ladies who wish to appear in " High

Court Dress" to obtain Royal permission, through the Lord Chamberlain.

This regulation does not apply to ladies who have already received permission to wear high dress.

White gloves only should be worn, excepting in case of mourning, when black or grey gloves are admissible.

As a lady on presentation does not now kiss the Queen's hand as formerly she did, she is not required to remove the right-hand glove before entering the Presence Chamber. This order, therefore, is no longer in force, and a lady wearing elbow gloves and bracelets will find it a great convenience not to be obliged to take off her glove.

It is compulsory for both Married and Unmarried Ladies to Wear Plumes. — The married lady's Court plume consists of *three* white feathers.

An unmarried lady's of *two* white feathers.

Feathers must be worn so that they can be clearly seen on approaching Their Majesties.

In deep mourning black feathers may be worn.

White veils or lace lappets must be worn with the feathers.

Coloured feathers were formerly adopted by many ladies; but the original regulations respecting wearing white plumes are now strictly enforced by Royal command.

Bouquets are not included in the dress regulations issued by the Lord Chamberlain, although they are invariably carried by both married and unmarried ladies. It is thus optional to carry a bouquet or not, and some elderly ladies carry much smaller bouquets than do younger ladies.

A fan and a lace pocket-handkerchief are also carried by a lady on presentation or on attending a Court, but these two items are also altogether optional.

CHAPTER XI

Levées are held by the King in person. Those who have been presented at levées held by His late Majesty, King Edward, do not require to be again presented to His Majesty King George.

Four or more Levees are usually held every year by the King at St. James's Palace.

Gentlemen are officially presented by the heads of any department or profession to which they individually belong, whether civil or military, naval or clerical; it is more usual for a gentleman to be presented by the head of his department, or by the colonel of his regiment, than by his nearest relative.

Presentations are also made by Relatives and friends of those presented; but these are greatly in the minority at all levées.

Gentlemen must be again presented at every step in their career, whether civil, military, naval, or clerical —on civil appointments, on gaining steps of naval, military, legal, or clerical rank, and on accession to title, whether inherited or conferred.

Those entitled to be presented at His Majesty's Levées are the members of the aristocracy and gentry, the members of the diplomatic corps, the Cabinet, and all leading Government officials, Members of Parliament, leading members of the legal profession, the naval and military professions, the leading members of the clerical profession, the leading members of the medical and artistic professions, the leading bankers, merchants, and members of the Stock Exchange, and persons engaged in commerce on a large scale. An exception to the rule as regards retail trade is made in favour of any person receiving Knighthood, or when holding the office of Mayor, or being made a Justice of the Peace, or on receiving a Commission in the Volunteer forces.

The dates on which levées are to be held are duly announced in the *Gazette*, and in the daily newspapers.

At all future levées cards of admission will be required, as the numbers at each of these ceremonies must be limited.

The Lord Chamberlain has issued the following revised list of rules, which are to be observed at attendances and presentations in future—

All officers, whether on the active or retired lists, of the Royal Navy and the Royal Marines, of whatever rank, should communicate with and obtain their cards from the private secretary to the First Lord of the Admiralty. All civil officers of the Admiralty should follow the same rule.

All officers, whether on the active or retired lists, of the Army, Militia, Yeomanry, or Volunteers, of whatever rank, except those on the Indian and Colonial Establishments, should communicate with and obtain their cards from the Adjutant-General at the War Office, stating clearly at which levée they desire to be present, and whether they wish to attend or to be presented; if the latter, stating by whom and on what occasion. Deputy lieutenants of counties should also communicate and obtain their cards from the War Office.

Officers of the Household Cavalry and Foot Guards on the active list should make application to the Lord Chamberlain at St. James's Palace for cards of admission and presentation. All retired Officers of the Household Cavalry and Brigade of Guards should apply to the War Office.

All officers of the Indian Civil Service and of the Indian Army, of whatever rank, whether on the active or retired lists, should communicate with and obtain their cards from the private secretary to the Secretary of State at the India Office, Whitehall.

All officers of the Colonial service and Colonial forces, of whatever rank, whether on the active or retired lists, should communicate with and obtain their cards from the Colonial Office, Whitehall.

Similarly, all gentlemen connected with the Foreign Office, the Home Office, officials connected with the Houses of Parliament, or any Government department, should communicate with and obtain their cards for attendance or presentation at levées from the department under which they serve.

Judges, law officers, King's counsel, and all legal officials holding appointments under the Crown are requested to make their applications through the secretary to the Lord Chancellor.

Peers, bishops, Lords-Lieutenants of Counties, Members of Parliament, clergy of all denominations, and all gentlemen, other than the above-mentioned, should communicate with the Lord Chamberlain at St. James's Palace, when they will each be furnished with a card of admission for use at the levée.

The names both for attendance and presentation must be received at the various offices above indicated not later than eight days prior to the date of each levée, but in the case of officers, who make application to the War Office, fourteen days before the date of each levée.

When a Gentleman makes a Presentation it is compulsory for him to attend the same levée as the person whom he presents, and the card of presentation is sent to him to be forwarded to the person to be presented.

A Gentleman on being presented should bow to the King, and His Majesty will bow to him in return. Gentlemen attending a levée should also bow to His Majesty.

Gentlemen who have been presented at a levée have the privilege of writing their names in His Majesty's visiting book at Buckingham Palace once during the season. The hours of calling for this purpose are generally from three to five o'clock in the afternoon.

As regards the Dress to be worn at Levées, full-dress uniform is invariably worn by all gentlemen entitled to wear it—officers of both Services, officers of the militia, volunteer officers, deputy-lieutenants, etc.

All officers of Scottish kilted corps, whether regulars, militia, or volunteers, should wear the kilt in Court dress, irrespective of their being mounted officers or not.

Officers on half-pay wear a regulation uniform and not the full-dress uniform of their regiment. Legal dignitaries wear their full-dress robes of office.

Archbishops, bishops, and clergy should appear in full canonicals, that is, black silk full- or pudding-sleeve gowns, cassock and sash bands, etc., with black breeches, silk stockings, shoes and buckles. The academical habit should not be worn at Court except when addresses are presented from the Universities.

Gentlemen not belonging to any profession, and strictly speaking civilians, wear Court dress, which is either of cloth or velvet, the former being more worn than the latter. When the suit is of cloth it consists of trousers of claret or of dark blue colour, with a narrow gold stripe down the side; a dress coat, single-breasted, with broad collar, cuffs, and pocket flaps, white waistcoat and white tie, cocked hat and sword. When the dress is of velvet the dress coat is usually ornamented with steel buttons; knee breeches, with silk stockings, shoes and buckles, are worn,

G

and not trousers. The cocked hat and sword should be worn in either case.

Old Court dress including silk waistcoat, lace ruffles, and bag wig is occasionally worn by elderly gentlemen.

Dark claret, dark blue, and dark brown are the colours usually worn by civilians when the suit is of cloth, and black when it is of velvet.

Gentlemen wear gloves when attending levées.

When the Court is in mourning, gentlemen attending a levée are expected to wear a band of black crape on the left arm above the elbow.

CHAPTER XII

Balls are given in town and country by society at large, and these invitation balls include Hunt Balls, Military and Naval Balls, Yeomanry and Territorial Balls, Bachelors' Balls, etc.

Public Balls are those balls for which tickets of admission can be purchased, although for many of these balls it is necessary to obtain vouchers from the committees or patronesses, when held in town or at watering-places.

Public balls include County Balls, Charity Balls, and Subscription Balls, etc.

In Town, Ball-giving is in a way a science, and an amusement upon which large sums of money are frequently expended.

A Crowded Ball is not always pronounced a good ball by the guests, often the contrary, but then, again, what is termed a thin ball is open to the accusation of not going off well, and falling rather flat; of not being kept up with spirit, and of being considered a stupid ball, and so on.

To hit upon a happy medium with regard to the number of guests is an achievement in ball-giving which is only arrived at by a careful study of the map of the county, and a judicious selection of night. This selection is of paramount importance to the success of a ball, as when a smarter ball is given at a smarter house on the particular evening chosen by the giver of a less brilliant ball, the grander ball extinguishes the lesser ball, through the most fashionable people merely looking in at the one, and remaining the rest of the evening at the other. This putting out as it were of the lesser light, occurs very frequently during the London season to ball-givers moving in the same sets. The guests who have been expected to add lustre to the lesser balls appear but for a few minutes, and usually arrive rather early, uncomplimentarily early, at perhaps a little before eleven, and remain hardly half an hour in the rooms, making their way to another ball of the same calibre, and remaining there perhaps another twenty minutes, before arriving at the goal, viz. *the* ball of the evening. Both ladies and gentlemen follow this practice, thus, at a little after twelve, an average ball-giver finds her rooms deserted by all but those who have nowhere else to go. Although the flitting of the guests thus early is a disappointment to the hostess, and although it does not prevent the fleeting ball-givers from making suitable returns by placing the family on their ball lists, it yet greatly mars the enjoyment of the ball, and prevents its being looked back upon with anything approaching to pleasure or satisfaction, the departure of the most eligible partners being not the least of the vexations of the night.

These *contretemps* are sometimes unavoidable ; but, when practicable, it is always best to postpone a ball rather than to allow it to clash with a ball of greater pretensions.

An impromptu dance is often a great success, while an impromptu ball is almost as certain to prove a great failure.

The Difference between a Dance and a Ball consists in the number of the invitations issued, in the strength of the band, and the extent of the supper arrangements.

At a dance the number of the guests varies from eighty to two hundred ; at a ball they vary from two hundred to five hundred.

At a dance a piano band is frequently engaged, while at a ball a full band is requisite. At a ball the floral decorations are a great feature, at a small dance they are often dispensed with. Ladies new to society as it were, or whose circle of acquaintance is of a limited character, and who do not number in that circle many ball-givers, and who yet desire to form a ball acquaintance, frequently place their ball in the hands of some intimate friend of higher standing than themselves, giving her *carte blanche* to form a ball list. When this plan is followed, invitations are still sent out by the ball-giver; in every case the name and compliments of the lady who forms the list are sent with the card.

This plan, although of advantage to the hostess, is often productive of much unpleasantness to her unfashionable friends, who are naturally very much affronted at being excluded from the ball list, which they usually are, as a lady who undertakes to form a ball list for a friend is not a little arbitrary as to the conditions under which she assumes its management. She naturally wishes the ball to be confined to her own set, to the exclusion of what she terms all outsiders.

Ladies are always more or less reluctant to yield up their ball to the exclusion of their old friends, however anxious they may be to make new ones. But when a ball is thus given it is thoroughly understood that conditions, however stringent, must be complied with.

A Hostess should receive her Guests at the head of the staircase at a ball given in town, and at the door of the ball-room at a country house ball. She should shake hands with each guest in the order of their arrival.

The ladies of a party should advance towards the hostess, followed by the gentlemen of their party.

A lady and gentleman should not ascend the staircase arm-in-arm, or make their entrance into the ball-room arm-in-arm. The gentlemen invariably enter the ball-room after the ladies of their party, and never before them, or arm-in-arm with them. A ball is usually opened either by the hostess herself, or by one of her daughters.

Opening a Ball simply signifies dancing in the first quadrille at the top of the room with a gentleman of highest rank present.

When a member of the Royal Family, or a foreign prince, is expected, dancing should not commence until the arrival of the royal guest; and when the royal guest is a lady, the host should open the ball with her, having his wife or daughter as *vis-à-vis*. When the royal guest is a prince, the hostess or her daughter should open the ball with him.

When a prince wishes to dance with any lady present, with whom he is unacquainted, his equerry informs her of the prince's intention, and conducts her to the prince, saying as he does so, " Mrs. A——, your Royal Highness " or " Miss B——, your Royal Highness." The prince bows and offers her his arm; the lady should curtsy and take it. She should not address him until addressed by him, it not being considered etiquette to do so. The same course is followed by a princess ; strangers to the princess should not ask her to dance, but the host has the privilege of doing so. When more than one royal personage is present, the one of the highest rank leads the way, with either hostess or host. (See Chapter V.)

Royal Guests should be received by the host and hostess at the entrance of the mansion, and by them conducted to the ball-room. At ball-suppers the same precedence is strictly in force, the royal guests leading the way with host or hostess (see p. 49).

The same etiquette should be observed on the departure of royal guests as on their arrival.

General Introductions should not be made to royal guests, and introductions should be made by request only.

Gentlemen present at a ball are expected to ask the daughters of the house for one dance at least.

A hostess should use her own discretion as to any introduction she thinks proper to make. When a ball is given in the country, the hostess should endeavour to find partners for those young ladies who are strangers to the general company. But when a ball is given in town, she is not expected to do so, as in town the guests are supposed to be acquainted with each other more or less, and to be independent of the kind offices of a hostess.

The Dances now in vogue are "Quadrilles," "Lancers," "Valses," "The Highland Reel," and the "Polka," and often a London ball concludes with a "Cotillon," in which expensive presents are given.

Country dances, such as "Sir Roger de Coverley," etc., are usually danced at private balls when given in the country.

The Precedency observed in sending guests in to supper is far more punctiliously followed in the country than in town. The host should take in the lady of highest rank present, and the hostess should endeavour to send in the principal guests according to their individual rank; but in town she generally leaves the guests to follow the host and lady of highest rank according to their inclinations, a guest should not enter the supper-room before the host has done so.

When a gentleman takes a lady in to supper, he should re-conduct her to the ball-room as a matter of course; the fact of friends joining her in the supper-room would not relieve him from this obligation. And the same etiquette applies equally to a lady. She should return to the ball-room only with the gentleman who has taken her down to supper, unless she is engaged for the ensuing dance, when her partner might come in quest of her; she should then return to the ball-room with him.

It is not usual for guests to take leave of a hostess at a London ball. This remark applies to acquaintances of the hostess, and not to intimate friends.

At a country ball the guests are on a more friendly footing than is generally the case in town; and, therefore, make a point of taking leave of the hostess if possible.

It is optional whether a host conducts a lady to her carriage or not. In the country more is expected of him than in town in this respect, as at a London ball, such a civility would involve a vast amount of exertion which few hosts would be willing to undergo : ladies accompanied by an acquaintance generally make their way to their carriages.

The Custom of covering in Small Balconies and the windows of the drawing-rooms where a ball takes place, rendering the atmosphere of the room almost insupportable from the total exclusion of air, is fast disappearing. The space gained by this means for the accommodation of the guests is totally disproportionate to the discomfort thereby entailed upon them.

Ball-givers have at length realised the mistake of crowding two hundred to three hundred people together into rooms not properly ventilated, and it is now the rule, when covering in balconies, to introduce window frames into the bunting covering, and to drape them with lace curtains, etc., the windows of the ball-room being entirely removed.

Large blocks of ice are frequently placed in convenient spots for the purpose of cooling the atmosphere, and coloured ice produces a pretty effect.

Patent ventilators are also much in use, and the substitution of electric lighting, on account of its emitting little heat, has become general.

Ball-goers appreciate these alterations as only those who

have experienced the close, stifling atmosphere of an over-
crowded ball-room can do, and as half the London ball-
rooms are only average-sized drawing-rooms, the absurdity
of excluding air from the ball-room with yards of thick
canvas cannot be too severely criticised.

Ball-givers, too, frequently issue far more invitations
than the size of their rooms authorises, under the mistaken
idea that to have a great crowd in their rooms is to give
a good ball.

But experienced ball-givers limit the number of their
invitations to under two hundred, instead of expanding it
to over three hundred.

The Country Ball Season ostensibly commences in
November, reaches its zenith in January, and terminates
early in February.

The stewards of these balls are, as a rule, the represen-
tatives of the various classes by whom they are attended;
the members of the aristocracy residing in the county
heading the list of stewards, and the members of the
professional classes usually closing it.

The top of the ball-room is, as a rule, appropriated
by the aristocratic element, head stewards and "lady
patronesses."

The enjoyment derived from country balls depends
upon a variety of circumstances, which do not influence in
a like degree the ball-going world of London.

County Balls are principally composed of a series of
large parties brought by different ladies in the neighbourhood where the ball is held; but there are two classes of
county balls, balls which are held in large and populous
towns and attended by the principal residents of the towns,
with only a small sprinkling of the county aristocracy and
county gentry.

There are also Hunt Balls and annual Charity Balls

which take place between October and February, and which are an amalgamation of both classes of balls.

The neighbourhood where a ball is held is a sufficient indication as to whether it is likely to be a smart one or not.

As a rule the leading ladies of a county lend their names as patronesses and supporters of a charity ball, although it by no means follows that they will personally attend it; but a long list of influential patronesses materially increases the sale of tickets, which is the result to be achieved.

A large attendance is not the primary object of a county ball, as the sum raised by the sale of tickets is only required to defray the expenses of the ball, although these are sometimes considerable, especially when the decorations are elaborate, and the arrangements on a grand scale, in which case there is not seldom a deficiency rather than a surplus, which deficiency is defrayed by the stewards themselves.

To ensure a good ball considerable unanimity on the part of the county ladies is demanded, and they usually meet and consult together previous to fixing the date of the ball, to take into consideration the fixtures of neighbouring county balls, and so avoid the possibility of the said balls clashing with their own county ball, and also with a view of perhaps attracting the house parties of their more distant neighbours to swell the numbers at their own ball.

House parties invited for a ball vary from ten to twenty-five, as the accommodation of a house admits.

It is not the province of the stewards of a ball to find partners for either ladies or gentlemen, and therefore, if a lady does not form one of a large party, but merely attends a county ball with a relative or friend, and has not a large acquaintance amongst these present, she has very little chance of obtaining partners.

Young ladies do not now return to their chaperons after each dance, or after they have been to the tea-room.

A couple should not stand arm-in-arm during the pauses in the figures of a quadrille, or while resting during a valse.

In round dances, it is customary to take frequent pauses, and not to race round the ball-room until the music ceases.

At country balls programmes are invariably used; at London balls they are never used, save at public balls.

County balls usually commence between nine and ten o'clock, sometimes a ball is not opened until the most influential of the stewards and their parties have arrived, but oftener than not the two first dances are over before the arrival of the county magnates.

It depends upon the length of the drive at what time people arrive at a ball; as a rule, they do not arrive later than 10.30 p.m.

The usual mode of conveying a house-party to a ball is by private omnibus in addition to carriages and motor cars; but when these are hired for the occasion the expense should be defrayed by the guests themselves.

It is usual to leave a country ball not later than half-past two; the most fashionable people invariably do so about that hour.

As a matter of course persons attending public balls take their ball tickets with them.

When attending a Military Ball, or a Hunt Ball, it is usually the rule to take the invitation card and hand it to the sergeant or official in attendance.

It is sometimes stated on the invitation card that this is to be done, although it is often taken for granted that persons will do so of their own accord.

At balls given by private individuals, the invited guests should not bring their invitation cards with them, unless in the case of a *bal masqué*, where they are sometimes requested to do so.

In giving a ball three weeks' notice is considered necessary, but with regard to a dance a short ten days' notice would suffice.

The Invitation Card is the usual "at home" card, the word "Dancing" being printed in the corner of the card.

The word "ball" should never be used on an invitation card, however grand the entertainment; and the same form of invitation is employed either in the case of a small dance or of a large ball, though in the event of a small dance only being given, the words "Small" or "Early" should be written or printed on the invitation card.

Invitations to a ball should be issued in the name of the hostess only.

When the host is a widower, with a grown-up daughter, the invitations should be issued in their joint names.

When the host is a widower, or a bachelor, they should be issued in his name.

Invitations issued by officers, members of hunt committees, bachelors, etc., to their balls, either request the pleasure or the honour of Mrs. ——'s company; but this formula should not be used by ladies when issuing invitations; the "at home" card should simply bear the word "Dancing" on the bottom of the card, the hour and date filled in in the allotted space, the name of the guest written at the top of the card.

In the case of a written invitation, it would be correct to use the words "ball" or "dance" when alluding to the entertainment about to be given, in a friendly note.

A lady or gentleman might ask for an invitation for his or her friend to a ball given by an acquaintance, although the acquaintanceship were of a slight character; but a lady or gentleman should not ask for an invitation to a ball if unacquainted with the giver of it. The fact of mutual friends having received invitations to a ball gives no claim upon the hospitality of a stranger, therefore such requests are inadmissible.

The proper course for a person to pursue in the event of desiring an invitation to a ball given by some one with whom he or she is unacquainted, is to request some mutual friend to obtain one; and this course is always followed.

Cards should be left by the guests present at a ball within the current week if possible. (See Chapter III.)

Gratuities should never be given by the guests to the servants of the house where a ball is given.

State Balls.—Two State Balls are annually given at Buckingham Palace during the London season by command of His Majesty. Invitations are issued by the Lord Chamberlain, but His Majesty previously revises the list.

When ladies and gentlemen attend a State Ball at Buckingham Palace they make their way to the ball-room *unannounced;* and there is no official reception accorded to them, either by " Royalty " or by the Lord Chamberlain.

Dancing does not commence until the arrival of the royal party, when the guests rise and remain standing while the Royal Quadrille—with which the ball opens—is being danced.

The King and Queen act as host and hostess on these occasions, but confine their attentions to those with whom they are personally acquainted.

Ladies attending a State Ball at Buckingham Palace should wear the usual full evening dress; but they should not wear Court trains, or plumes, or lappets.

Gentlemen attending State Balls should wear uniform or full Court dress—dress coat, breeches and silk stockings, shoes and buckles; trousers can only be worn as part of a uniform, and not with a Court dress as generally worn at a levée.

A gentleman intending to dance should remove his sword, otherwise he should not do so.

When the Court is in mourning, ladies attending a State Ball should wear mourning according to the official notice which duly appears in the *Gazette.*

Gentlemen should wear crape on the left arm, which is supplied in the cloak-room of the Palace to those who have forgotten to provide themselves with it, as it is imperative, when the Court is in mourning, that a band of crape should be worn at either State Ball or State Concert.

The balls given by the princes and princesses of the blood royal are not State Balls, therefore Court dress is not worn by the gentlemen present.

They act as host and hostess at the balls given by them and receive their guests, shaking hands with them as they are announced.

Ladies and gentlemen do not take their cards of invitation with them to Buckingham Palace.

CHAPTER XIII

Dinner giving is perhaps the most important of all social observances, therefore dinner parties rank first amongst all entertainments.

Dinner giving is so thoroughly understood to rest upon the principle of an equivalent, that those who do not give dinners hardly come within the category of diners out. This rule, however, is open to many exceptions in favour of privileged individuals, popular and prominent members of society whose presence at dinner parties is appreciated and welcomed in most circles.

Dinner-parties are of more frequent occurrence, and are of more social significance, than any other form of entertainment.

Dinner Invitations.—An invitation to dinner conveys a greater mark of esteem, or friendship and cordiality, towards the guest invited, than is conveyed by an invitation to any other social gathering, it being the highest compliment, socially speaking, that is offered by one person to another. It is also a civility that can be readily interchanged, which in itself gives it an advantage over all other civilities.

The orthodox dinner giver must necessarily possess a certain amount of wealth, and wealth and wit do not always go hand in hand. Oftener than not, the former rather overweights the latter ; hence, the introduction of a lighter element in the form of amusing people whose *métier* in life it is to be amusing and to appear amused.

Dinner giving is in itself not only a test of the position occupied in society by the dinner giver, but it is also a direct road to obtaining a recognized place in society. A means of enlarging a limited acquaintance and a reputation for giving good dinners is in itself a passport to fashionable society. Dinner giving, in the fullest sense of the word, is a science not easily acquired, so much depending on the talent which the host or hostess may possess for organizing dinner-parties.

When a large dinner-party is contemplated, it is usual to give three weeks' notice, but of late this notice has been extended to four, five, and even six weeks.

Diners out are rather inclined to rebel against this innovation, considering that an invitation bearing the date of a month hence pledges them to remain in town, and as it were controls their movements, for the acceptance of an invitation is in the eyes of diners out a binding obligation; only ill-health, family bereavement, or some all-important reason justifies its being set on one side or otherwise evaded.

Those inconsiderate enough to make trivial excuses at the last moment are not often retained on the dinner-list of a host or hostess.

Dinner invitations are issued in the joint names of host and hostess.

The master of the house occupies a prominent position amongst his guests, when dispensing hospitality as a "dinner giver."

From five to ten days' notice is considered sufficient for invitations to small and unceremonious dinner-parties.

Printed cards are in general use in town for issuing dinner invitations, and can be purchased from any stationer; these cards only require to be filled in with the names of host and hostess and guests, date, hour, and address. The united names of the host and hostess should be written in the space left for that purpose. Thus, "Mr. and Mrs. A.," and the name or names of the guests in the next vacant space.

When invitations are issued for small dinner-parties, it is more usual to write notes than to make use of printed cards.

Acceptances or refusals of dinner invitations should be sent with as little delay as possible after the invitations have been received. It is a want of courtesy on the part of a person invited not to do so, as a hostess is otherwise left in doubt as to whether the person invited intends dining with her or not, and is consequently unable to fill up the vacant place with an eligible substitute; thus rendering her dinner-party an ill-assorted one.

An answer to an invitation cannot be solicited in a subsequent note; it is therefore incumbent upon the invited person to dispatch an answer within a day or two at least. Dinner invitations are either sent by post or by a servant, and the answers are also conveyed in a like manner.

Dinner invitations are invariably sent out by the hostess.

It is not usual in town to invite more than three members of one family; it is now the custom to ask young ladies with their parents to dinner-parties.

Receiving Dinner - Guests. — The guests should arrive within fifteen minutes of the hour named on the invitation card.

On no occasion is punctuality more imperative than in the case of dining out; formerly many allowed themselves great latitude in this respect, and a long wait for the tardy guests was the result. A host and hostess frequently waited over half an hour for expected guests. But now punctuality has become the rule in the highest circles, and dinner is served within twenty minutes of the arrival of the first guest. In general, people much given to dining out make a point of arriving in good time; but there are many in society who presume upon their position, and are proverbially unpunctual, knowing that in the height of the season

H

a hostess would wait half an hour rather than sit down to dinner without them; but this want of consideration soon becomes known in their different sets, and is always taken into account when "their company is requested at dinner."

In France, it is not the rule, or the custom, to wait dinner for late arrivals, and the dinner is served punctually to the hour named in the invitation.

The dinner-hour varies from eight to nine, although perhaps 8.30 is the most usual hour. In the country it ranges from 7.30 to 8.30.

Punctuality on the part of the guests enables the hostess to make any introductions she may consider advisable before dinner is served.

The host and hostess should be in readiness to receive their guests in the drawing-room at the hour specified on the card.

On arrival, a lady should take off her cloak in the cloak-room, or should leave it in the hall with the servant in attendance, before entering the drawing-room.

A gentleman should leave his overcoat and hat in the gentlemen's cloak-room, or in the hall.

At large dinner-parties, the butler is stationed on the staircase, and announces the guests as they arrive. At small dinner-parties, or where only one man-servant is kept, the servant precedes the guest or guests on their arrival, to the drawing-room. The guests should then give their names to the servant, that he may announce them.

A lady and gentleman, on being announced, should not enter the drawing-room arm-in-arm or side by side. The lady or ladies, if more than one, should enter the room in advance of the gentleman, although the servant announces "Mr., Mrs., and Miss A."

The host and hostess should come forward and shake hands with each guest on arrival. The ladies should at once seat themselves, but gentlemen either stand about the room and talk to each other, or sit down after a wait of some minutes.

When a lady is acquainted with many of the guests present, she should not make her way at once to shake hands with all, but should make an opportunity to do so in an unobtrusive manner; it would be sufficient to recognise them by a nod or a smile in the mean time. A lady should bow to any gentleman she knows, and he should cross the room to shake hands with her at once if disengaged.

At a small dinner-party, where the guests are un-acquainted, the hostess should introduce the persons of highest rank to each other; but at a large dinner-party, she would not do so, unless she had some especial reason for making the introduction.

In the country, introductions at dinner-parties are far oftener made than in town.

Precedency is strictly observed at all dinner-parties. (See Chapter V.)

Sending Guests in to Dinner.—The host should take the lady of highest rank present in to dinner, and the gentleman of highest rank should take the hostess. This rule is absolute, unless the lady or gentleman of highest rank is related to the host or hostess, in which case his or her rank would be in abeyance, out of courtesy to the other guests.

A husband and wife, or a father and daughter, or a mother and son, should not be sent in to dinner together.

A host and hostess should, if possible, invite an equal number of ladies and gentlemen. It is usual to invite two or more gentlemen than there are ladies, in order that the married ladies should not be obliged to go in to dinner with each other's husbands only. Thus, Mrs. A. and Mr. B., Mr. B. and Mrs. A., Mrs. B. should be taken in to dinner by Mr. C., and Mr. A. should take Mrs. G., and so on.

When ladies are in a majority at a dinner-party to the extent of two or three, the ladies of highest rank should be taken in to dinner by the gentlemen present, and the remaining ladies should follow by themselves; but such an arrangement is unusual and undesirable, though sometimes unavoidable when the dinner-party is an impromptu one, for instance, and the notice given has been but a short one.

If there should be one gentleman short of the number required, the hostess frequently goes in to dinner by herself, following in the wake of the last couple.

The usual mode of sending guests in to dinner is for the host or hostess to inform each gentleman, shortly after his arrival, which of the ladies he is to take in to dinner.

No "choice" is given to any gentlemen as to which of the ladies he would prefer taking in to dinner, it being simply a question of precedency.

Should any difficulty arise as to the order in which the guests should follow the host to the dining-room, the hostess, knowing the precedency due to each of her guests, should indicate to each gentleman when it is his turn to descend to the dining-room. He should then offer his arm to the lady whom the host had previously desired him to take in to dinner.

Dinner is announced by the butler or man-servant.

When the guests have arrived, or when the host desires dinner to be served, he should ring or inform the servant accordingly.

On dinner being announced, the host should give his right arm to the lady of highest rank present, and, with her, lead the way to the dining-room, followed by the lady second in rank, with a gentleman second in rank and so on. The gentleman of highest rank present should follow last with the hostess.

When the second couple are about to leave the drawing-room, the hostess frequently requests each gentleman in turn to follow with a lady according to the precedency due to each. Thus, "Mr. A., will you take Mrs. B.?" This also answers the purpose of an introduction, should the couple be unacquainted with each other, and the hostess has not found an opportunity of introducing them to each other on their arrival.

When a case of precedency occurs, in which either the lady or gentleman must waive their right of precedence, that of the gentleman gives way to that of the lady. (See Chapter V.)

A gentleman should offer his right arm to a lady on leaving the drawing-room.

Ladies and gentlemen should not proceed to the dining-room in silence, but should at once enter into conversation with each other. (See the work entitled "The Art of Conversing.")

On entering the dining-room the lady whom the host has taken in to dinner should seat herself at his right hand. On the Continent this custom is reversed, and it is etiquette for the lady to sit at the left hand of the gentleman by whom she is taken in to dinner.

The host should remain standing in his place, at the bottom of the table, until the guests have taken their seats, and should motion the various couples as they enter the dining-room to the places he wishes them to occupy at the table. This is the most usual method of placing the guests at the dinner-table. When the host does not indicate where they are to sit, they sit near to the host or hostess according to precedency.

The host and hostess should arrange beforehand the places they wish their guests to occupy at the dinner-table.

If a host did not indicate to the guests the various places he wished them to occupy, the result would probably be that husbands and wives would be seated side by side, or uncongenial people would sit together.

The custom of putting a card with the name of the guest on the table in the place allotted to each individual guest is frequently followed at large dinner-parties, and in some instances the name of each guest is printed on a menu and placed in front of each cover.

The host and the lady taken in to dinner by him should sit at the bottom of the table. He should sit in the centre at the bottom of the table and place the lady whom he has taken down at his right hand. The same rule applies to the hostess. She should sit in the centre at the top of the table, the gentleman by whom she has been taken in to dinner being placed at her left hand.

The lady second in rank should sit at the host's left hand.

Each lady should sit at the right hand of the gentleman by whom she is taken in to dinner.

It is solely a matter of inclination whether a lady and gentleman, who have gone in to dinner together, converse with each other only, or with their right- and left-hand neighbours also, but they usually find some topic of conversation in common, otherwise a dinner-party would prove but a succession of *tête-à-tête*.

The Menus are placed the length of the table, on an average one to two persons or occasionally one to each person, and the menu cards are elaborate or simple, according to individual taste, and are purchased printed for the purpose, having a space for the names of the dishes to be filled in, which is usually done by the mistress of the house, unless the establishment is on a large scale, it being usual to write them out in French.

Fanciful menu holders are much in use.

The use of menus would be pretentious at a small dinner-party when there is but little choice of dishes; but when there is a choice of dishes a menu is indispensable.

The Usual and Fashionable Mode of serving Dinner is called *Dîner à la Russe*, although at small or friendly dinners the host sometimes prefers to carve the joint himself in the first course, and the birds in the second course. But dinner-tables, whether for dining *à la Russe*, or for dining *en famille*, are invariably arranged in the same style, the difference being merely the extent of the display made as regards flowers, plate and glass, which are the accessories of the dining-table.

When the host helps the soup, a small ladleful for each person is the proper quantity; a soup-plate should not be filled with soup.

When the party is a small one, and the joints or birds are carved by the host, the portions should be handed to the guests in the order in which they are seated, although occasionally the ladies are helped before the gentlemen.

The rule at all dinner-parties is for the servant to commence serving by handing the dishes to the lady seated at the host's right hand, then to the lady seated at the host's left hand, and from thence the length of the table to each guest in the order seated, irrespective of sex.

Double *entrées* should be provided at large dinner-parties, and the servants should commence handing the dishes at both sides of the table simultaneously.

Dîner à la Russe is the Russian fashion introduced into society many years ago. The whole of the dinner is served from a side-table, no dishes whatever being placed on the table save dishes of fruit.

Dinner-table Decorations.—As regards the most correct style of dinner-table decorations, they offer great diversity of arrangement.

High centre pieces and low centre pieces. Low specimen glasses placed the length of the table and trails of creepers and flowers laid on the table-cloth itself are some of the prevailing features of the day, but table decorations are essentially a matter of taste rather than of etiquette, and the extent of these decorations depends very much upon the size of the plate chest and the length of the purse of the dinner giver.

The fruit for dessert is usually arranged down the centre of the table, amidst the flowers and plate. Some dinner-tables are also adorned with a variety of French conceits besides fruit and flowers; other dinner-tables are decorated with flowers and plate only, the dessert not being placed on the table at all; but this latter mode can only be adopted by those who can make a lavish display of flowers and plate in the place of fruit.

For the purposes of lighting, lamps or silver candelabra with wax candles are used, according to the wealth of the dinner giver. Both lamps and candles are usually shaded with coloured shades, as they produce a pretty effect, and prevent the guests being incommoded by too close a proximity to the glare occasioned by some dozens of candles or by brilliant lamps; therefore, shades are considered indispensable.

Electric light and electric lamps are now greatly the fashion, and offer many advantages.

The term " cover " signifies the place laid at table for each person, and for such arrangements see chapter " Waiting at Dinner " in the work entitled " Waiting at Table."

When liqueurs are given they are handed after the ices.

Sherry is always drunk after soup, hock either with oysters before the soup or with the fish after the soup, and Chablis sometimes takes the place of hock. Champagne is drunk immediately after the first *entrée* has been served, and so during the remainder of dinner until dessert. Claret, sherry, port, and Madeira are the wines drunk at dessert, and not champagne, as it is essentially a dinner wine.

Dinner-table Etiquette.—Soup should be eaten with a table-spoon and not with a dessert-spoon, it would be out of place to use a dessert-spoon for that purpose. Dessert-spoons, as their name implies, are intended for other purposes, such as for eating fruit-tarts, custard-puddings, etc., or any sweet that is not sufficiently substantial to be eaten with a fork; but whenever a fork can be used it is best to use it.

Fish should be eaten with a silver fish-knife and fork.

All made dishes, such as *quenelles*, *rissoles*, patties, etc., should be eaten with a fork only, and not with a knife and fork.

For sweetbreads and cutlets, etc., a knife and fork are requisite; and, as a matter of course, for poultry, game, etc.

In eating asparagus, a knife and fork should be used, and the points should be cut off and eaten with a fork as is sea-kale, etc.

Salad should be eaten with a knife and fork; it is served on salad plates, which are placed beside the dinner-plates.

Cucumber is eaten off the dinner-plate, and not off a separate plate.

Peas should be eaten with a fork.

In eating game or poultry, the bone of either wing or leg should not be touched with the fingers, but the meat cut close off the bone; and if a wing it is best to sever it at the joint, by which means the meat is cut off far more easily.

Pastry should be eaten with a fork, but in the case of a fruit tart, a dessert-spoon should be used as well as a fork, but only for the purpose of conveying the fruit and juice to the mouth; and in the case of stone fruit—cherries, damsons, plums, etc.—either the dessert-spoon or fork should be raised to the lips to receive the stones, which should be placed at the side of the plate; but when the fruit stones are of larger size, they should be separated from the fruit with the fork and spoon, and left on the plate, and not put into the mouth; and whenever it is possible to separate the stones from the fruit it is best to do so.

Jellies, blancmanges, iced puddings, etc., should be eaten with a fork, as should be all sweets sufficiently substantial to admit of it.

When eating cheese, small morsels of the cheese should be placed with the knife on small morsels of bread, and the two conveyed to the mouth with the thumb and finger, the piece of bread being the morsel to hold, as cheese should not be taken up in the fingers, and should not be eaten off the point of the knife.*

The finger-glass should be removed from the ice-plate and placed on the left-hand side of the dessert-plate. When ices are not given, the d'oyley should be removed with the finger-glass and placed beneath it.

When eating grapes, the half-closed hand should be placed to the mouth, and the stones and skins allowed to fall into the fingers, and placed on the side of the plate. Some persons bend the head so as to allow of the stones and skins of the grapes falling on the side of the plate; but this latter way is old-fashioned, and seldom followed. Cherries and other small stone-fruit should be eaten in the way grapes are eaten, also gooseberries.

When strawberries and raspberries, etc., are not eaten with cream, they should be eaten from the stalks; when eaten with cream, a dessert-spoon should be used to remove them from the stalks. When served in the American fashion without stalks, both fork and spoon should be used.

Pears and apples should be peeled and cut into halves and quarters with a fruit-knife and fork, as should peaches, nectarines, and apricots.

Melons should be eaten with a spoon and fork.

Pines with knife and fork.

The dessert is handed to the guests in the order in which the dinner has been served.†

When the guests have been helped to wine, and the servants have left the dining-room, the host should pass

---

* Respecting the arrangement of the dinner table for dessert, see the work entitled "Waiting at Table."

† See the work entitled "Waiting at Table."

the decanters to his guests, commencing with the gentleman nearest to him.

It is not the fashion for gentlemen to drink wine with each other either at dinner or dessert, and the guest fills his glass or not, according to inclination.

Ladies are not supposed to require a second glass of wine at dessert, and passing the decanters is principally for the gentlemen. If a lady should require a second glass of wine at dessert, the gentleman seated next to her would fill her glass; she should not help herself to wine. After the wine has been passed once around the table, or about ten minutes after the servants have left the dining-room, the hostess should give the signal for the ladies to leave the dining-room, by bowing to the lady of highest rank present, seated at the host's right hand. She should then rise from her seat, as should all the ladies on seeing her do so.

The gentlemen should rise also, and remain standing by their chairs until the ladies have quitted the room, which they should do in the order in which they have entered it, the lady of highest rank leading the way, the hostess following last.

The host, or the gentleman nearest the door, should open it for the ladies to pass out, and close it after them.

When the ladies have left the dining-room, the gentlemen should close up as near to the host as possible, so as to render conversation general.

The wines usually drunk by gentlemen after dinner are claret of a fine quality, and port.

The ladies on leaving the dining-room return to the drawing-room. Coffee should be almost immediately brought to the drawing-room. The coffee-cups containing coffee should be brought on a silver salver, with a cream-jug and a basin of crystallised sugar.

In large country houses coffee is sometimes brought in a silver coffee-pot, and the lady would then pour out her own coffee, the servant holding the salver the meanwhile.

Coffee should be taken a few minutes later to the dining-room, and either handed to the gentlemen, or placed on the table, that they may help themselves (see the work previously referred to).

A very general plan is, after the wine has gone round once or twice, for the host to offer cigarettes, which are smoked before the gentlemen join the ladies in the drawing-room.

After coffee, the gentleman of highest rank should leave the dining-room first. The host would not propose an adjournment to the drawing-room, until he observed a wish to do so on the part of his guests, but there is no hard and fast rule on this head.

It is not now the fashion for gentlemen to sit over their wine beyond fifteen or twenty minutes at the utmost, instead of as formerly, from three-quarters of an hour to an hour, a change much appreciated by hostesses.

On the Continent the gentlemen accompany the ladies to the drawing-room, and do not remain in the dining-room as in England.

The gentleman of highest rank present could suggest an adjournment to the drawing-room within a quarter of an hour if he thought proper to do so. If the other guests were engaged in a discussion in which he did not wish to take part, having suggested the adjournment, he could leave the dining-room to join the ladies in the drawing-room; but as a rule, the gentlemen leave the dining-room together, the host following last.

The host should ring the dining-room bell before leaving the room, as an intimation to the butler that the gentlemen have left the room.

At ceremonious dinner-parties in town neither music nor cards are introduced during the usual half-hour passed in the drawing-room before the hour for departure.

At country-house dinner-parties music or round games of cards are in request.

Departure after Dinner.—There is no rule as to the order in which the guests should take their leave. Half-past ten is the usual hour for general departure; and the butler announces the several carriages as they arrive to the guests in the drawing-room. But if any lady wished to inquire if her carriage had arrived, she should ask the hostess's permission to do so; and the bell would be rung for the purpose of making the enquiry. The same remark applies to ordering a cab: the lady should ask the hostess if one might be ordered for her.

The hostess should shake hands with all her guests on their departure, rising from her seat to do so.

Each guest on departure should shake hands with both host and hostess.

If, on leaving the room, acquaintances should pass each other, they should wish each other good-night, but they should not make the tour of the rooms for the purpose of so doing.

The host should conduct one or two of the principal of his lady guests to their carriages.

The ladies should put on their cloaks in the cloak-room, the host waiting in the hall meanwhile.

A gentleman related to the host or hostess, or a friend of the family, could offer to conduct a lady to her carriage if the host were otherwise engaged.

Gratuities should never be offered by the guests at a dinner-party to the servants in attendance. Gentlemen should not offer fees to the men-servants, neither should ladies to the lady's-maid in attendance.

The guests should call on the hostess within a week or ten days after a dinner-party. If "not at home," a married lady should leave one of her own cards and two of her husband's; a widow should leave one of her own cards; a bachelor or a widower should leave two cards.

The rule as to calling after dinner-parties is greatly

relaxed between intimate friends, and the call often omitted altogether; and this more particularly as regards gentlemen, whose occupations during the day are considered good and sufficient reasons for not calling.

Country Dinner-parties.—In the country, new acquaintances, if neighbours, should be asked to dinner within a month of the first call if possible, and the return invitation should be given within the following month.

When guests are assembled at a country house, they are sent in to dinner, on the first evening, according to their individual precedence; but on subsequent evenings the gentlemen frequently draw lots to decide which lady they shall have the pleasure of taking in to dinner, otherwise a lady and gentleman would go in to dinner together five or six consecutive times, according to the length of the visit, but this is more a practice with people who march with the times, than with what are termed " old-fashioned people."

When a party is varied by additional dinner-guests each evening, drawing lots gives way to precedency, it being too familiar a practice to be adopted at a large dinner-party.

Saying Grace, both before and after 'dinner,' is a matter of feeling rather than of etiquette. It used to be very much the custom to say "grace," but of late years it is oftener omitted than not, especially at large dinner-parties in town.

In the country, when a clergyman is present, he should be asked to say grace. When grace is said by the host, it is said in a low voice, and in a very few words; the guests inclining their heads the while.

It was no rapid revolutionary change in manners that brought about the difference that now exists between the Elizabethan and Victorian eras; no polished mentor came forward to teach that it was not the nicest and cleanest thing to do, to put knives into the salt, to dip fingers into plates, or to spread butter with the thumb ; on the contrary, these things righted themselves little by little, step by step, until the present code of manners was arrived at. But it is quite possible that a hundred years hence it will be discovered that the manners of the present century offered wide scope for improvement.

In the meantime these rules of etiquette observed in society are adhered to and followed by those who do not wish to appear singular, eccentric, old-fashioned, unconventional, or any other adjective that the temper of their judges may induce them to apply to them for committing solecisms, either small or great.

Married Ladies, as a rule, dine out with their Husbands, and do not accept invitations to large dinners when their husbands are unable to accompany them. There are, of course, exceptions to this rule, and circumstances sometimes arise when it is greatly relaxed ; but even in this case it would be in favour of small and friendly dinners rather than large ones.

During any temporary absence of her husband, a lady would accept invitations to dine with her relatives and intimate friends, though she might refuse invitations to large dinners given by acquaintances ; but, as a rule, when it is well known that the head of a house is away for any length of time, invitations are seldom sent to the wife by givers of large dinners.

When young ladies are invited to dinner they accompany their father, mother or brother ; but occasionally, when a young ladies' party is given by a friend of their parents', the young ladies are invited alone, and they should either go with their maid in a cab or by themselves in their father's carriage.

CHAPTER XIV

FASHION has its freaks and its vagaries, and in relation to inanimate objects these freaks and vagaries are but transitory and evanescent, but when they touch upon manners and modes they become a conventionality and a custom perhaps for many a year. Changes and innovations, slight as they are, are more subtle than sudden, and, paradoxical as it may seem, they are as important as they are insignificant; still it is difficult to believe that fingers once did duty for forks, and that it was not customary for a host to supply his guests with forks, who, if fastidious enough to require them, were expected to bring them in their pockets.

There are here and there people in society who affect a few eccentricities of manner, but these whims at all times take the form of originalities and not of vulgarities; and even then are only indulged in by those whose position in society is secure.

As regards Dinner-table Etiquette.—When a lady has taken her seat at the dinner-table, she should at once remove her gloves; although occasionally long elbow gloves are not removed during dinner, but this is conspicuous and inconvenient. She should unfold her serviette and place it on her lap. It is immaterial whether she places the bread on the right or left-hand side of the cover when taking it from the serviette.

A gentleman should do the same with his serviette and

bread, placing the one across his knees, and the other at his right or left hand.

When a lady is some little time taking off her gloves, she should remove her serviette before doing so : otherwise a servant would offer her soup before she had made room for the soup-plate by removing the serviette, and she should decide quickly as to which of the two soups handed to her she will take, so as not to keep the servant waiting ; and so on through every course throughout the dinner as regards fish, meat, etc.

The guests should consult the menu on first sitting down to dinner. Eating soup comes first under notice. In olden days it was customary to drink it out of a basin. In these days no one " drinks " soup, it is " eaten "; whether it be mock turtle or the clearest julienne, it is eaten out of a soup-plate at dinner, and with a table-spoon.

There is a reason for this choice of spoons; soup is nothing if it is not hot, and as it is the custom to give only about half a ladleful to each person, it is eaten quicker, and therefore hotter, with a large spoon than with a small one.

There is also a good and sufficient reason for small quantities of soup being given in lieu of large ones, viz. the extent of the menu; and when a plateful of soup is handed to a guest accustomed to the regulation supply, he fears that he is expected to dine off it, and that there is nothing much to follow.

Again, small helpings require a smaller quantity of soup to be provided, and a servant is less likely to spill plates containing a little soup than plates that are half full.

At ball suppers, when soup is served in soup-plates, it is also eaten with a table-spoon, but not when served in small cups.

Many years ago it was fashionable to eat fish with a fork and a crust of bread; previous to this a table-knife and fork were considered the proper things to use for this purpose. It was then discovered that a steel knife gave an unpalatable flavour to the fish, and a crust of bread was substituted for the knife. This fashion lasted a considerable time, in spite of the fingers being thus brought unpleasantly near to the plate, and to this day old-fashioned people have a predilection for that crust of bread. One evening a well-known diner-out discarded his crust of bread, and ate his fish with two silver forks; this notion found such general favour that society dropped the humble crust and took up a second fork. This fashion had its little day, but at length the two forks were found heavy for the purpose and not altogether satisfactory, and were superseded by the dainty and convenient little silver fish-knife and fork which are now in general use.

Small pieces of fish should always be given, and two different sorts of fish should not be placed on the same plate.

When oysters are given they precede the soup, and should be eaten with a dinner-fork, not with a fish-fork. In eating oysters the shell should be steadied on the plate with the fingers of the left hand, the oysters should not be cut, but should be eaten whole. Very many ladies do not eat oysters at dinner simply because they do not like them, while others refuse them under the impression that it is more ladylike not to eat them. Perhaps with regard to young ladies it is a taste to be acquired. Some men are very, if not over, fastidious, about the appetites displayed by ladies, and would have them reject the *entrées* and dine upon a slice of chicken and a spoonful of jelly. Others, on the contrary, respect a good appetite as giving proof of good health and good digestion. There is of course a medium in all things, and as large dinners are ordered mainly with a view to please the palates of men with epicurean tastes, it is not expected that ladies should eat of the most highly seasoned and richest of the dishes given, but should rather select the plainest on the menu. This remark more particularly applies to young ladies and young married ladies, whilst middle-aged and elderly ladies are at liberty to do pretty much as they please, without provoking comment or even observation.

With reference to entrées, some are eaten with a knife and fork, others with a fork only. All *entrées* that offer any resistance to a fork require the aid of both knife and fork, such as cutlets, *filet de bœuf*, sweetbreads, etc., but when rissoles, patties, quenelles, boneless curry, *vol-au-vents*, timbales, etc., are eaten, the fork only should be used.

In the case of the lighter *entrées*, the contact of the knife is supposed to militate against their delicate flavour; thus, for these *bonnes bouches* the fork is all-sufficient wherewith to divide and eat them.

The leg of a chicken, pheasant, duck, or wild duck should never be given to a guest save on those occasions when there are more guests present than there is meat from breasts and wings to offer them. Under these circumstances the carver is reduced to the necessity of falling back upon the legs of the birds, but in this case only the upper part of the thigh should be given, thus a guest has little difficulty in cutting the meat from the bone. A wing of a bird is usually given to a lady. Formerly it was thought a correct thing to sever the wing at the joint and then to cut the meat from the bone; but this requires a certain amount of strength in the wrist, and dexterity, should the bird not be in its *première jeunesse.*

As regards small pigeons, golden plovers, snipe, quails, larks, etc., a whole bird is given to each guest, and the proper way to eat these birds is to cut the meat from the breast and wings and to eat each morsel at the moment of cutting it; the bird should not be turned over and over on the plate, or cut in half or otherwise dissected. The legs of Bordeaux pigeons are not, as a rule, eaten, and half a bird only is given, as there is sufficient on the wing and breast to satisfy an ordinary second-course appetite. When the legs of smaller birds are eaten, such as snipe or golden plover, the meat should be cut off as from the breast or wing.

Young girls, as a rule, seldom eat a second course delicacy of this description; a little chicken or pheasant on the contrary is usually accepted by them.

When large potatoes are served in their skins a salad-plate should be handed at the same time whereon to place them.

When asparagus first comes into season it is often given in the second course instead of in the first, in which case it is eaten as a separate dish. When handed with meat or poultry it should be eaten on the same plate containing either.

In eating asparagus, some elderly gentlemen still adhere to the fashion of their youth and hold the stalks in their fingers, but the younger generation cut off the points with a knife and fork.

Seakale also is given in the second course when first in season, and should be eaten with a knife and fork.

Mushrooms are also eaten with a knife and fork.

It need hardly be said that it would be a vulgarity to eat peas with a knife, although those who reside abroad, or who are in the habit of travelling on the continent, are not unaccustomed to seeing this done by foreigners who are well-bred men.

Artichokes are, it may be said, an awkward and untidy vegetable to eat; they are only given in the second course as a separate vegetable; the outside leaves should be removed with the knife and fork, and the inner leaves which surround the heart, or head of the artichoke should be conveyed to the mouth with the fingers and sucked dry; epicures consider this vegetable a dainty morsel, but at dinner-parties young ladies should not attempt to eat these artichokes.

Savouries, when possible, should be eaten with a fork, but occasionally a knife also is of imperative use.

As regards sweets, *compôtes* of fruit and fruit tarts should be eaten with a dessert-spoon and fork, as should those dishes where juice or syrup prevails to the extent of rendering a dessert-spoon necessary. But whenever it is possible to use a fork in preference to a spoon it is always better to do so.

Jellies, creams, blancmanges, ice puddings, etc., should be eaten with a fork.

As a matter of course, young ladies do not eat cheese at dinner-parties.

CHAPTER XV

Evening Parties are styled receptions or "at homes" according to the number of guests invited. In official and political circles they are invariably styled "Receptions," but when given on a smaller scale in general society they are styled "At Homes."

Invitations to evening parties should be issued on "at home" cards.

The name of the person invited should be written at the top of the card at the right-hand corner, the words "at home" being printed beneath the name of the lady issuing the invitation, the day and date beneath the words "at home," the hour beneath the date. The address should be printed at the bottom of the card.

When music is to be given it should be mentioned on the "at home" card, thus, "Music."

The hour varies from 10 to 11 o'clock; in private circles 10 or 10.30 is the usual hour; in official circles 10.30 or 11 o'clock.

When a foreign royal personage is expected, or a foreigner of distinction, or a personage possessing public interest, the words "To meet Her Serene Highness Princess D.," or "To meet Count C." should be written at the top of the invitation cards.

When a reception or "at home" follows a dinner-party given by the hostess, it is not usual to provide any special amusement for the guests. But when an "at home" does not follow a dinner-party, it is usual to provide some sort of amusement for the guests, such as professional vocal or instrumental music.

The guests are expected to arrive from half an hour to an hour of the time mentioned on the invitation card, although it is optional when they do so.

Receiving the Guests.—The hostess should receive her guests at the head of the staircase, where she usually remains until the principal of her guests have arrived; while the host welcomes the guests in the drawing-room itself.

Receptions or "at homes" usually terminate shortly before one o'clock, save on Saturdays, when the hour of departure is 12 o'clock precisely.

Making Introductions.—A hostess should use her own discretion as regards making introductions.

When a royal personage is present the most distinguished of the guests should be presented by the host or hostess. When a celebrity is present introductions should also be made; and as regards general introductions they should be made whenever the hostess judges it expedient to do so, and the principal guests when unacquainted should be introduced to each other when the opportunity occurs.

Going in to Supper.—The host should take the lady of highest rank in to supper.

When a royal princess is present the host should take her in to supper.

When a royal prince is present he should take the hostess in to supper. (See Chapter V.)

It is optional whether the hostess follows with the gentleman of highest rank present, unless a foreign prince is present, when she should follow the host, and in the case of a royal prince being present she should precede the host.

When a royal prince or princess or a serene highness is present a table should be set apart for the host and hostess and royal party, and any among the guests whom the royal visitors may desire should join them at supper.

When the supper-room is not sufficiently large to accommodate the whole of the guests at the same time, the most distinguished guests should go in first.

When the host is informed that supper is served he should tell the principal gentlemen present which of the ladies he wishes them to take into supper, and should himself lead the way with the lady of highest rank present.

The hostess should also assist in sending the principal guests in to supper, and when the general company observe the move towards the supper-room, they should follow in the same direction.

When the general company are apparently not aware that the supper-room is open, the hostess should ask the various gentlemen to take the ladies in to supper, and should herself lead the way with one of the gentlemen.

When the general company find the supper-room crowded they should return to the drawing-room for a quarter of an hour or so ; but the hostess should arrange for some instrumental or vocal performance to commence when supper is first served, so as to occupy the attention of the guests who remain in the drawing-room.

The guests frequently do not return to the drawing-room after supper, but go to the cloak-room for their cloaks and wraps, and thence to their carriages.

It is not usual to take leave of the host and hostess at receptions.

Royal Guests present.—When a royal personage is present the host should conduct her to her carriage.

When a foreign prince is present the host should accompany him to the hall door.

Tea and Light Refreshments should be served during the evening in the library, or in an adjacent apartment.

Supper should be served at twelve o'clock, in the dining-room, and should be similar in character to a ball supper.

Invitations to Bridge Parties are issued on "at home" cards when the guests number upwards of forty, and on visiting cards when a lesser number is invited.

The Invitation Form is, "Mrs. A—— At Home" in both instances. The day, date, and hour are put beneath the words "at home," and "Bridge" in the corner of the cards opposite the address. The usual hour for holding these evening receptions is 9 o'clock p.m., which allows of three hours' play before midnight. The guests arrive very punctually, rather before than after the hour named on the invitation cards. The guests comprise an equal number of both sexes, as husbands and wives are invited together when both are known to be bridge players, and bachelors who do not disdain playing for small stakes are in great request. Also unmarried ladies of a certain age; not girls in their teens.

Prizes are given in some houses to the conquering players. One for the ladies and one for the gentlemen, and occasionally a second prize for the second best player of either sex. This is done when playing for money does not commend itself to a host and hostess. The prizes consist for the most part of useful articles. For instance, a box of gloves, a box of bonbons, a case of eau d'Cologne, a card-case, a bag purse, and so on, all of which are acceptable to ladies; and a box of cigars or cigarettes, a silver pocket-flask, a silver-mounted stick or umbrella, are prizes the men winners are pleased to accept.

The Bridge Tables at which the guests are to sit are numbered, and the hostess arranges by whom they are to be occupied. The names—four in number for each table—are written or printed with the number of the table upon small cards and given to the guests by the hostess on arrival. This is done that good players may be placed together, and to save confusion and loss of time in seating them at the various tables.

The Refreshments provided consist in the first instance of "coffee," which is brought into the card-room or drawing-room and handed to the guests. No eatables are given with this after-dinner coffee. A supper is given either at the conclusion of the play at 12 o'clock—this being the more usual plan—or at 10.30, after which play is resumed for another hour or so; but the latter is more of a provincial custom than a town one, and is intended for those whose dinner hour is an early one—6.30, perhaps.

When a supper is not given, very good light refreshments are substituted for it, including cups of hot soup in the winter months.

Going in to Supper is arranged as far as possible on the following lines, if precedence does not prevent its being carried out. The players at each table who are partners when supper is served go in together. The host leads the way with his partner, and all follow, the hostess and her partner going last.

Cards should be left within a week or ten days after a reception.

A married lady should leave one of her own and two of her husband's cards.

A widow should leave one of her own cards.

A bachelor or widower should leave two of his cards. (See Chapter III.)

CHAPTER XVI

Afternoon Weddings have become very popular with all classes, 2.30 o'clock being the usual hour for their being solemnised, and only very quiet weddings take place in the morning hours. Formerly, it was only the few who were in a position to obtain special licences who could have afternoon weddings.

Marriage by " Banns " is greatly in favour in general society. The banns must be published three consecutive weeks previous to the marriage in the parish in which the bridegroom resides, and also in that in which the bride resides, and both should reside fifteen days in their respective parishes previous to the banns being published.

Marriages by Licence.—When a marriage is solemnised by licence the cost, with fees and stamps, amounts to £2. This should be obtained at the Faculty Office, or at the Vicar-General's Office, Doctors' Commons, and is available at any church in the parish where one of the parties has resided for fifteen days previous to the application being made for the licence, either in town or country.

When the licence is obtained in the country through a clerical surrogate the cost varies, according to the diocese, from £1 15s. to £2 12s. 6d.

Special Licences can only be obtained from the Archbishop of Canterbury, after application at the Faculty Office, and an especial reason must be given for the application, and one that will meet with the Archbishop's approval.

The fees for a special marriage licence average £29 5s. 6d.

The Fees to the officiating clergymen vary considerably, according to the position and means of the bridegroom, from £1 1s. to £5 5s., as the inclination of the bridegroom may dictate.

The fee to the clerk is subject to a like variation, commencing at 10s.

All fees relating to a marriage should be defrayed by the bridegroom, and paid by him, or by the best man on his behalf, in the vestry of the church, previous to the ceremony or immediately after it.

The Etiquette observed at Weddings is invariably the same whether the wedding takes place in the morning or in the afternoon, or whether it is a grand wedding or a comparatively small one, whether the guests number two hundred or whether they number twenty.

The Invitations should be issued from three weeks to a fortnight before the wedding-day.

The wedding luncheon or wedding reception should be given by the parents of the bride or by her nearest relative, and the invitations should be issued in the names of both parents.

The invitations should be issued in notes printed in ink; they are now seldom printed in silver. The form should be as follows : " Mr. and Mrs. —— request the pleasure of Mr. and Mrs. ——'s company at the marriage of their daughter Helen with Mr. John S——, at St. Peter's Church, Hanover Square, on Tuesday, May 8th, at 2.30 o'clock, and afterwards at —— Square. R.S.V.P."

If a stepdaughter, it should be " at the marriage of Mrs. A——'s daughter Helen B——."

Wedding Presents.—Every one who is invited to a wedding invariably makes the bride or bridegroom a present; it is the received rule to do so. Many send presents before the invitations are sent out—as soon as the engagement is made known, if it is not to be a long one.

There is no rule as to the time before the wedding-day when the present should be sent; but invitations are usually sent to those who have given presents, even though they live at a considerable distance, and may not be able to attend the wedding.

Wedding presents are displayed on tables of various sizes, according to their number, and if very numerous and valuable, it is not unusual to exhibit them at an afternoon tea, given for the purpose on the day previous to the wedding. Each present should bear the card of the giver attached to it. Presents of silver plate should be placed on a table covered with dark cloth or velvet. It is not unusual to surround the presents with flowers, notably roses, and this is often done by persons of artistic tastes.

The Bridegroom should provide the wedding-ring and the bridal bouquet.

The bouquets for the bridesmaids are also the gift of the bridegroom, and should be sent to them on the morning of the wedding. He is also expected to make a present to each bridesmaid—either a brooch, a locket, a bracelet, or a fan, which should either be sent the day before the wedding or on the morning of the wedding-day.

The bridegroom should provide the carriage to convey himself and his bride from the church to the house where the wedding luncheon and reception are to take place, and again from the house to the railway-station, or, if the journey is made by road, to the place of honeymoon; but frequently the bride's father places his own carriage or motor-car at the disposal of the bride and bridegroom for this purpose, especially in the country. The bridal carriage

is the only one, according to etiquette, which the bridegroom is expected to provide.

The invited guests should provide their own carriages,
and neither the bridegroom nor the bride's father are ever
expected to do so. This should be thoroughly understood
by the guests in every case.

The custom of having groomsmen to support the bridegroom is now very general, as at royal weddings, a royal
bridegroom being supported by from four to six groomsmen. Two of the groomsmen usually act as ushers and
assist in seating the guests.

The Best Man should be a bachelor, although a
married man could act in this capacity. He should either
accompany the bridegroom to the church or meet him there.
He should stand at his right hand during the ceremony—a
little in the rear—and should render him the trifling service
of handing him his hat at the close of it.

He should sign the register afterwards in the vestry, and
should pay the fees to the clergyman, clerk, etc., on behalf
of the bridegroom, either before or after the ceremony, if
the bridegroom does not pay them on arrival.

The bridegroom and best man should arrive at the
church before the bride, and await her coming, standing
at the right-hand side of the chancel gate.

The Bride should be driven to the church in her father's
carriage. If she has a sister or sisters, and they officiate as
bridesmaids, they, with her mother, should precede her to
the church. The carriage should then return to fetch the
bride and her father; but when she has no sisters, her
father generally precedes her to the church, and receives
her at the church door, her mother accompanying her in
the carriage.

The bridesmaids should arrive some little time before
the bride, and form a line on either side of the church

porch, or within the church doorway. The mother of the bride usually stands beside them.

When the bride arrives she should take her father's right arm, or the right arm of her eldest brother or nearest male relative, who is deputed to give her away; he should meet her at the church door in the place of her father, and conduct her to the chancel or altar.

The Bridesmaids should follow the bride and her father up the nave of the church, walking "two and two" when the number of bridesmaids is even, four, six, eight, or twelve; but when the number is odd, as five, seven, or nine, and three of them happen to be children, which is generally the case, the elder bridesmaids should walk "two and two," following next after the children.

At fashionable weddings one or two little boys act as pages, and occasionally bear the bride's train.

The head bridesmaid is generally the bride's eldest unmarried sister or the bridegroom's sister, and she should follow next to the bride with her companion bridesmaid, when children are not included in the group.

The Bride's Mother should follow next to the bridesmaids; she should take her son's arm, or the arm of some near relative, in following them up the nave of the church. But ladies and gentlemen seldom walk arm-in-arm at a wedding, unless a lady requires the assistance of a gentleman in making her way quickly through the throng to her carriage at the conclusion of the ceremony, in which case it is quite correct to do so.

The Bride's Immediate Relatives and the near relatives of the bridegroom should seat themselves in pews or chairs, according to the church in which the service is celebrated. In some churches the service takes place at the entrance of the chancel, and the bridal party enter the chancel and stand at the altar to receive the address, and the concluding portion of the service only is there celebrated.

The Bridegroom's Relatives should place themselves on entering at the right of the nave, thus being on the bridegroom's right hand, and seat themselves in pews. The relatives of the bride should place themselves on entering at the left of the nave, thus being on the bride's left hand, and seat themselves in pews or chairs. Large cards with the words " For the Relatives of the Bridegroom," " For the Relatives of the Bride," are frequently placed in the pews to indicate where they are to sit.

The Bride should stand at the bridegroom's left hand ; the bride's father, or nearest male relative, should stand at her left hand, in order to give her away.

The bridesmaids should stand immediately behind the bride in the order in which they pass up the church.

The bride should take off her gloves at the commencement of the service and should give them with her bouquet to the head bridesmaid to hold.

The invited guests should sit in the pews or chairs.

Guests seldom take their prayer-books with them to the church to follow the service therefrom. The hymns sung are usually printed on leaflets, and placed in the pews or on the seats.

The bridegroom generally wears a flower in his buttonhole, as he does not wear a wedding favour.

The other gentleman may, as a matter of course, wear button-hole bouquets, if they please.

When the Service is concluded, the bride should take the bridegroom's left arm, and, preceded by the officiating clergyman, and followed by her head bridesmaids, father, mother, and the most distinguished of the guests, should enter the vestry, where the register should

K

be signed by the bride and bridegroom, two or three of the nearest relatives, and by two or three of the most intimate of the friends, and principal of the guests, including the best man and the head bridesmaid. The bride's father should sign it, but it is optional whether the bride's mother does so or not.

When the register has been signed, and those in the vestry have shaken hands with the bride and offered their congratulations, the bride should take the bridegroom's left arm and pass down the nave of the church followed by her bridesmaids, in the same order as they have previously passed up the nave. The most usual way now is for the bride and bridegroom to leave the church without pausing to shake hands with any of their friends present.

When the bride and bridegroom have driven off from the church, the bride's mother should be the next to follow, that she may be at home to receive the guests as they arrive. There is no precedence as to the order in which the remainder of the company leave the church; it entirely depends on the cleverness of their servants in getting up the carriages.

The Wedding Favours should be in the meantime distributed by the bridesmaids to the guests, in the vestry and in the church. Button-hole bouquets of natural flowers have, however, superseded the old-fashioned wedding favours for both ladies and gentlemen, and should be offered to the guests before they leave their seats at the conclusion of the ceremony. Wedding favours should be worn on the left side, by both ladies and gentlemen.

A Bride who is a Widow should not wear a bridal veil, nor a wreath of orange-blossoms, nor orange-blossom on her dress.

She should not be attended by bridesmaids, and wedding favours should not be worn by the guests.

How the Invitations to the Wedding Reception of a Widow should be issued depends upon individual circumstances. For instance, if a young widow resides with her parents, the invitations should be issued in their names as at her first marriage, and the form of invitation should be similar, save that the words " Their daughter, Mrs. A., widow of the late Mr. A." should be substituted for her christian name. If, as is oftener the case, a widow resides in her own house, or if the marriage is to take place from an hotel, the invitations should be issued in her own name, and the form should be " Mrs. Cecil A. requests the pleasure (or the honour) of Mr. and Mrs. B.'s company at her marriage with Mr. Henry C., at St. George's Church on Tuesday, December 30th, at 2.30 o'clock, and afterwards at Eaton Gardens, R.S.V.P." " The presence of" instead of "the company of" may be put if preferred.

It is understood that a Widow should not have Bridesmaids, but it is open to her to have the attendance of pages, if a wedding is to be a fashionable and smart one, although many ladies do not avail themselves of this privilege. The bridegroom should have a best man, as a matter of course; he may be the bride's brother if desired (the idea that this is not permitted is an erroneous one). A married man might be asked to act in the capacity of best man, there being no bridesmaids to require his attention, although this is seldom done, and a bachelor brother or friend is preferred.

A Widow may be given away by her father, uncle, brother, or even by a friend; indeed, it is more usual to have this support than not. At a first marriage " to be given away" is imperative, at a second it is optional; and if a widow at a quiet wedding prefers not to follow this custom she can do so.

Much Uncertainty exists as to whether a Widow should or should not continue to wear her First Wedding Ring when she marries a second time. In point of fact there is no hard and fast rule with regard to it, and a widow may continue or not continue to wear it, as she feels inclined. If she has children, and has had some years of married life, she usually retains it. If she is a young widow, she is likely to remove it, and wear the second ring only; but when this is her intention, she should not cease to wear it until she has arrived at the church, and has taken off her gloves previous to the ceremony; but, take it all in all, it is more usual to wear the two wedding rings than the second one only.

Formerly, Widows considered it Imperative to be married in Widow's Colours, grey or mauve, and that white was forbidden wear; but it is no longer so regarded, and a widow may and does wear white or cream on her wedding-day—not exactly a maiden bridal dress, as a tinge of colour is introduced. The larger number still regard pale grey or pale heliotrope as more suitable on the occasion of a second marriage, and doubtless this is so when a widow is not in her first youth. A widow may not, of course, wear a bridal veil; she must wear a hat or toque, white or coloured, as she pleases. She can have a bouquet, not of white flowers only, but mauve or pink, or violets, according to choice. It is quite permissible to have a full choral service, and for the church in which the ceremony is performed to be decorated with plants and flowers, but wedding favours should not be given to the guests at its conclusion.

A Newly Married Pair should receive their Guests standing together at the reception. The bride's mother, or near relative, could assist them in receiving. If a luncheon is to be given, they should lead the way to the dining-room, and sit at the head of the table, side by side ; but if a reception tea is given, the guests might be sent in at the tea hour—that is to say, told that tea is going on, and the bride and bridegroom could follow later should the numbers be too great to admit of all going into the tea room at the same time.

It is quite in Order for a Widow to have a Wedding Cake, but it should not be decorated with orange blossoms or with white flowers, merely with icing and ornamentations. The display of presents at the marriage of a widow is, as a rule, a very restricted one. The bridegroom and the bridegroom's family being the principal donors, the presents are seldom exhibited. The exception is when a widow has made many new friends, and has received wedding presents from them. Presents, when made to a widow having a house of her own, are expected to be of substantial value, and there is a general reluctance felt to offering her trifles, even if expensive ones, such as a] girl-bride would appreciate ; not so a married lady of social standing.

On arriving at the House where the wedding luncheon or reception is to be held, the gentlemen should leave their hats in the hall. The ladies should not remove their bonnets or hats at a wedding luncheon or reception, neither should the bridesmaids do so.

Gentlemen should take off their gloves at wedding luncheons, but it is optional whether ladies do so or not.

At receptions it is optional with both ladies and gentlemen whether they take off their gloves or not.

The guests who have not already had an opportunity of speaking to the bride and bridegroom, on being ushered into the drawing-room, where the company assembles, should shake hands with them, having first gone through that ceremony with the host and hostess, if they have not already done so.

Previous to luncheon being announced the bride's father or mother should tell the principal of the gentlemen present whom to take down to luncheon. But this only applies to a sit-down luncheon.

At standing-up luncheons the guests are not sent in in couples, but go in as they please, even two or three ladies together, and little or no precedency, bridal or otherwise, is followed as a general rule.

The luncheon should be served in the dining-room, library, or large marquee, as the case may be.

The bride's mother and the bridegroom's mother should take precedence of all other ladies present on the occasion of a wedding luncheon.

At strictly Family Gatherings the Guests should go in to Luncheon in the following order :—The bride and bridegroom. The bride's father with the bridegroom's mother. The bridegroom's father with the bride's mother. The best man with the head bridesmaid. The remaining bridesmaids with the gentlemen who are to take them in to luncheon.

The rest of the company should follow in the wake of the bridesmaids. The bride should take the bridegroom's left arm.

Sitting-down luncheons and standing-up luncheons are equally fashionable, although the latter are far more general, and little or no bridal precedency is observed. When a standing-up luncheon is given, small tables are arranged for the convenience of the bridal party on one side of the room, while a long table occupies the centre of the room.

When a sitting-down luncheon is given the bride and bridegroom should sit either at the head of a long table or at the centre of it—the bride at the bridegroom's left hand. The bride's father should sit next the bride with the bride-

groom's mother. When the bride and bridegroom sit at
the centre of the table the bridesmaids should sit opposite
to them with the gentlemen who have taken them in to
luncheon; each sitting at a gentleman's right hand.

When the bride and bridegroom occupy the head of the
table, the bridesmaids, with the gentlemen who have taken
them in to luncheon, should place themselves next the
parents on either side of the table, dividing their number
into two groups.

When the bride's father is dead, her eldest brother or
nearest male relative should take his place and should take
the bridegroom's mother in to luncheon.

A Wedding Breakfast is now termed a luncheon,
champagne and other wines take the place of tea and coffee,
which beverages are not served until towards the end of
the luncheon. At weddings which take place at 2.30 p.m., a
luncheon is frequently given at 3, followed by a " tea " at 4.

The Luncheon Menu generally comprises soup,
entrées both hot and cold; chickens, game, mayonaises,
salads, jellies, creams, etc., etc., and other dishes of a like
character.

The sweets should be placed on the table, fruit also.

The entrées, etc., should be handed by the servants, the
sweets should also be taken off the table by the men-servants
and handed round in turn.

At a standing-up luncheon the gentlemen should help
the ladies and themselves to the various dishes on the
table, as dishes are not handed at this description of
luncheon; hot entrées and soup are not given. The menu
is in other respects similar.

The tables should be decorated with flowers at either
a standing-up or a sitting-down luncheon. Bottles of
champagne should be placed the length of the table at a
standing-up luncheon; if not, the gentlemen should ask the

servants in attendance for champagne for the ladies they have taken down, and for themselves. At a sitting-down luncheon the servants offer champagne to the guests in the same order in which they hand the dishes.

When the sweets have been handed the bride should cut the wedding-cake. This she does by merely making the first incision with a knife ; it should then be cut by the butler into small slices, and handed on dessert plates to the guests.

The Health of the Bride and Bridegroom should then be proposed by the most distinguished guest present, for which the bridegroom should return thanks. He should then propose the health of the bridesmaids, for which the best man should return thanks.

Occasionally the gentleman of highest rank present also proposes this health in place of the bridegroom.

The health of the bride's father and mother should be proposed by the bridegroom's father.

It is now the custom to confine proposing healths at wedding luncheons within the narrowest limits. The health of the bride and bridegroom, and that of the bridesmaids being, in general, the only healths proposed.

At standing-up luncheons and at wedding receptions, the health of the bride and bridegroom only is proposed.

The Bride should leave the Dining-room immediately after the healths have been drunk, to change her dress for departure.

The head bridesmaid should accompany her, if related to her, and the guests should adjourn to the drawing-room to await the bride's reappearance, which should not be long delayed, and the adieus should then be made. Leave-takings should not be prolonged more than is absolutely necessary.

The parents should follow the bride and bridegroom into the hall, and adieus to them should there be made.

The Old-fashioned Custom of throwing satin slippers after the bride is sometimes observed, foolish as it is. It is the best man's or the head bridesmaid's privilege to perform this ridiculous act.

When rice is thrown after a bride it should be scattered by the married and not by the unmarried ladies present; but since the publication of a former work in which these practices were discouraged they have been greatly discontinued.

Strewing the Bride's Path with Flowers from the church to the carriage by village children is a custom much followed at weddings which take place in the country.

The Honeymoon now seldom lasts longer than a week or ten days. Many brides prefer spending their honeymoon in their future home, if it happens to be in the country, instead of making a hurried trip to Paris or elsewhere, or to spending it at the country house of a friend, lent to them for the purpose. But it is entirely a matter of individual feeling which course is taken.

The Bride's Trousseau should be marked with the initials of the name she is to take.

The Bridegroom should provide the house-linen and all other things appertaining to the bride's new home.

The Wedding Presents should be dispatched to the bride's residence immediately after the wedding, and they should at once be put into their several places, and not arranged for the purpose of being shown to visitors.

The Bridal Wreath should not be worn after the wedding-day. The bridal wreath, the bridal bouquet, and the orange blossoms from the wedding-cake, if treasured as mementos of the happy event, should be preserved in the recesses of a locked drawer in the bride's chamber, and not exhibited under glass shades in the drawing-room.

Precedence should not be accorded to a bride during the first three months after marriage, although this old-fashioned custom is sometimes followed at country dinner-parties on the occasion of a bride's first visit.

The Custom of sending Wedding Cake to friends is an exploded one, and only followed between near relations.

Wedding Cards are, strictly speaking, out of date, and only sent by people who adhere to old-fashioned customs.

The Words "No Cards" should not be inserted when the announcement of a marriage is sent to the newspapers; neither should the intimation be added that the bride and bridegroom will be "at home" on certain days.

CHAPTER XVII

An Afternoon Wedding usually takes place between 2 and 2.30 o'clock, and the "at home" that follows is given from 2.30 to 5, on the return from church.

The words "at home" and the hour should be on the invitation card, also the name of the church and the hour fixed for the marriage.

Invitations to wedding receptions are no longer issued on "at home" cards, but are included in the invitations to the wedding ceremony issued in printed notes. (See Chapter XVI.)

The arrangements in the tea-room, and the refreshments given, should be similar to those provided at large afternoon "at homes," with the addition of wedding-cake and champagne.

Ceremony is, as far as possible, dispensed with as regards sending the guests into the tea-room, and this is a great advantage gained over a wedding luncheon, either a sitting-down or a standing-up one, when people are doubtful as to the exact place belonging to each individual relative.

The bride and bridegroom either enter first, followed by the bridesmaids and a few of the principal guests, or they follow later, as they prefer. The remainder of the company should make their way downstairs as space permits, for a wedding reception is a crowded affair, even in the largest of mansions. Not only is every one invited who has given a wedding present to either bride or bridegroom, within visiting distance, but even others who are not intimate enough to be expected to do so.

The guests should not make their way in the first instance to the tea-room, but should proceed at once to the drawing-room and shake hands with the host and hostess, and afterwards with the bride and bridegroom. The bride and bridegroom should stand together within the drawing-room and shake hands with all those with whom they are acquainted. The bride and bridegroom should be the first to enter the tea-room. Flowers, as a matter of course, are a great feature at wedding receptions.

The tea and coffee should be served by the maid-servants, generally by the lady's maids, but men-servants should also be in attendance to open the champagne as required. Very little wine is drunk at this hour of the day. Ladies seldom care for it, and gentlemen avoid it on principle. Still, out of compliment to the bride, the relatives quaff a cup of sparkling wine, although her health is seldom proposed or speeches of any kind made. The bride should put the knife into the wedding-cake, and the butler should cut it up and hand it to the guests.

Seats should not be placed in the tea-room, and the tables should occupy the top or side, or both the top and side, of the room, according to the number of guests invited, so as to leave as much space as possible in the centre of the room.

The bride and bridegroom are not always present at a wedding tea, as the departure for the proposed place of honeymoon does not in every case admit of it, and the mother holds the "at home," and the guests inspect the presents after the newly-married couple have left.

An "at home" is sometimes given a few days previous to the wedding for the inspection of the presents, if they are very numerous and beautiful; but even when this is done they still form a centre of interest on the afternoon of the wedding to the many guests. When jewellery and plate to any great extent form a portion of the presents, it is sometimes thought necessary to have a policeman on duty while the house is open to so many comers, and when to effect an entrance under the pretext of business would be an easy matter.

CHAPTER XVIII

The Responsibilities of a Bridegroom from a pecuniary point of view commence from the moment of his engagement. He must at once present the bride-elect with an engagement ring. A man of even moderate wealth finds no difficulty in choosing and purchasing a handsome ring costing from £50 to £100; but a poor man, possessing but a small income, is often put to more expense than he can conveniently afford in the matter of an engagement ring. He knows all the members of the bride's family will sit in judgment upon it if it is but a poor bauble worth about £10, which is quite as much as he feels he is justified in spending; he knows that both it and himself will be regarded as very mean, or as conveying a not very inspiriting prospect of days to come. The engagement ring worn on the bride's finger after marriage is a lasting memento, and if a poor one she will not be proud of it—neither will he. Rich men take the brides to choose engagement rings, expense being no object to them; but poor men cannot do this, as the choice might fall on gems beyond their means, therefore they make the choice themselves, according to the position of the families they are about to enter. If the standing is above their own, from a money point of view, the engagement rings have to be chosen in accordance with the jewels worn by members of such families, and a bridegroom would thus spend £40 at least on an engagement ring suitable to a lady so placed.

On the other hand, when men with small incomes marry
the daughters of parents of a similar position to their own,
the engagement rings given are not costly ones, and a ten-
pound note, or even less, would cover the cost of these
binding tokens. The wedding rings are within the means
of all bridegrooms, be they ever so poor.

During the Engagement the question of presents
to the brides-elect is never absent from the thoughts of
their bridegrooms. The wealthy please themselves and
their brides by giving costly jewels, which are often chosen
by the brides themselves in company with their bridegrooms. This is very delightful shopping, but it does not
fall to the lot of the great majority. Men of moderate
means give presents of moderate value and few in number;
they are not bound by etiquette during their engagements
to give any jewellery if their incomes do not warrant this
outlay; but a man must have very little money to go upon
if he cannot contrive to give a bracelet or necklet or some
such trinket to the girl he is about to marry.

To give Presents to the Bridesmaids is another
of the obligations of bridegrooms. Here again, the wealthy
exercise their generosity and good taste with the con-
currence of their brides, who assist them in the choice of
suitable presents in articles of jewellery. These average
£5 and upwards for each bridesmaid, which bring it to a
good total when the bridesmaids are numerous. The point
that affects the generosity of bridegrooms, however, is not
how much they ought to spend on these presents, but
rather, how little may be spent upon them with due consideration for the fitness of things, viz. the position of the
bridesmaids. Two sovereigns would be a reasonable sum
for a man of small means to spend on each gift to the
bridesmaid.

The Bridal Bouquet and the Bridesmaids' Bouquets come next on the list of expenses a bridegroom defrays. Rich men spend liberally in this direction, but average sums to give to meet ordinary incomes are two guineas to one guinea for a bride's bouquet, and five and twenty to fifteen shillings each for the bridesmaids' bouquets.

The Fees connected with the Ceremony are strictly the province of the bridegroom to defray. If a marriage is by licence, he pays the cost, which in town amounts to £2 2s. 6d., and in the country from £2 12s. 6d. to £3 3s. The fee to the vicar of the church where the marriage is to be solemnised varies from £1 1s. to £5 5s., oftener £1 1s. than not with the majority of bridegrooms with moderate incomes, the exception being £5 5s. The minor fees are very trifling that a bridegroom is expected to pay. He pays the organist for playing a wedding march at the conclusion of the service, if it is not a choral one; the bell-ringers look to him for their fee, as do the vergers, etc. Thus a bridegroom pays for what is absolutely necessary at the marriage ceremony only, and very little besides.

When a Friend of the Bride or Bridegroom performs the Ceremony or assists at it a fee is not given to him by the bridegroom, but a present of some kind is made to him, either in silver plate or by a small cheque, as circumstances dictate, for railway expenses or otherwise. It is usual for the bridegroom to do this unless the clergyman in question is a relative of the bride, when a joint present is usually given by bride and bridegroom.

The Bride's Parents bear a Large Share of the Wedding Expenses, foremost of which is the bride's trousseau, the cost of this being entirely dependent on position and income. The dinners and "at homes" given before the marriage to introduce the bridegroom to the members of the bride's family are given by the bride's parents. The wedding reception is given by them, either at their own residence or at an hotel. As concerns their share of the expenses connected with the ceremony, it depends upon whether the wedding is to be a smart one or a quiet one. If the former, the expenses that fall to them are somewhat considerable; if the latter, they are almost nil. A choral service, for instance, is paid for by the bride's parents, the organist, choirmaster, and choir all being severally paid by them. If the hymns sung are printed on leaflets this trifling expense also is included. All floral decorations are paid for by the bride's parents, as is the hire of the awning and the red felt at the church doors. When wedding favours or buttonholes are given it is by them also.

For whom the Bride's Family are expected to provide Carriages is invariably a Misunderstood Detail.—The bride's father has only to provide carriages or cars to convey himself and bride to the church, and for those members of his family residing under his roof, and for visitors staying with him for the wedding. He is not required to provide carriages for any other of the guests, save in the country, and then only for those who arrive by train at a roadside station and cannot obtain conveyances for themselves. In town the bridegroom has to provide the carriage to convey himself and bride from the church to her father's house, and afterwards to the station. In the country the reverse is the case, and the bride's father does this by lending one of his own carriages or cars for the purpose.

The Bridegroom is expected to provide the Furniture and all household effects for the new home, including plate and linen, which latter naturally form very important items. Many of the bridal presents, however are made to lighten these expenses, and consist of plate to

L

a great extent, and occasionally of linen also, from the members of the bride's family ; still, the rule in England is that the bridegroom should provide it as part of the necessaries of the home, and the gift of it by relatives is altogether optional.

CHAPTER XIX

Afternoon "At Homes" are a great feature amongst
the entertainments of the day, large afternoon parties, and
small afternoon parties; parties so large that the number
of guests equals those at a big crush or evening reception,
and so small that they might fairly come under the denomination of afternoon teas.

At afternoon "at homes," ladies are present in a
considerable majority, there being usually from about ten
gentlemen to thirty ladies on an average present at these
gatherings. Ladies have a decided partiality for this class
of entertainment, as it affords an opportunity for meeting
their friends and acquaintances, or for making new
acquaintances, and for forming future plans and inter-
changing civilities; and even in the height of the London
season, afternoon "at homes" are fully attended by the
members of the fashionable world.

There are various classes of afternoon "at homes":
the large "at home" of from fifty to two hundred guests,
when usually professional vocal and instrumental talent is
engaged, and fairly good music given, although the entertainment is not of sufficient importance to be termed a
concert; the "at home" of from fifty to a hundred guests
when only amateur talent is in requisition; and the small
"at home" of from ten to thirty people, when conversation
usually takes the place of music, the party being composed
of friends rather than of acquaintances.

Invitations to "At Homes" should be issued in the name of the hostess only, and not in the united names of the master and mistress of the house.

Invitations should be issued on "at home" cards, large and small, and also on visiting cards. The name of the person invited should be written at the top of the card at the right-hand corner, the words "at home" being printed beneath the name of the lady issuing the invitation, and the day and date beneath the words "at home," and the hour beneath the date. Any amusement to be given should be added at the bottom of the card at the left-hand corner. The address should be printed at the right-hand corner at the bottom of the card.

The letters R.S.V.P. are occasionally either written or printed on the "at home" card, at the left-hand corner of the bottom of the card, but it is not usual to write "R.S.V.P." in the corner of an afternoon "at home" card, as it is immaterial how many guests are present at this class of entertainment; but if an answer is so requested, an answer should be sent. R.S.V.P. signifies "*repondez, s'il vous plaît*," or "an answer is requested."

It is customary to include the head of the family, either husband or father, in the invitation. Thus, at the top of the card, at the right-hand corner should be written "Mr. and Mrs. A.," or "Mr. and Miss A." The daughters of the house should be included in the invitation sent to their mother. Thus "Mr. and Mrs. A.," "The Misses A.," but the sons of the house should be invited separately.

When a family consists of a mother and daughters, the invitation should be "Mrs. and the Misses A."

The title of "Honourable" should not be put on an invitation card, but only on the envelope containing the card.

All other titles are recognised on invitation cards; but the letters K.C.B., M.P., etc., should not be written on the cards, but only on the envelopes in which they are enclosed.

If a lady is aware that she will be unable to be present, it would be polite to send her excuses, although strict etiquette does not demand it; both the invitation and the answer can in all cases be sent by post.

It is not now considered necessary to leave cards after afternoon "at homes."

Invitations to large afternoon "at homes" should be issued a fortnight previous to the day, and to small "at homes" within a week or so of the day.

The Arrival of Guests.—When invited guests arrive, they should not inquire if the hostess is at home, but at once enter the house; and they should be ushered at once into the tea-room.

The gentlemen should leave their hats and overcoats in the hall.

At large "at homes" a cloak-room should be provided, so that a lady could remove a cloak or fur-cape, usually worn during the winter weather; but at small "at homes" a cloak-room is not necessary, as the reception-rooms are neither so crowded nor so warm, neither are the ladies' toilettes so elaborate.

Refreshments.—At large "at homes" refreshments should be served in the dining-room, on a long buffet at one end of the room, or on a long table the length of the room.

The lady's-maids and other maid-servants should stand behind the table to pour out and hand the cups of tea or coffee across the table as asked for.

It is usual to have women-servants on these occasions to pour out the tea, a man-servant or men-servants being also in attendance, in case anything is required of them, although gentlemen usually help themselves to claret-cup, wine, etc.

The usual refreshments given at these "at homes" are

tea and coffee, the latter served from large silver urns. (See chapter "Preparing Afternoon Tea," in the work entitled "Waiting at Table.") Sherry, champagne-cup, claret-cup, ices, fruit, fancy biscuits and cakes, thin bread-and-butter, potted game, sandwiches, etc.

Ice plates are used for ices, dessert plates for fruit and fruit salads.

At small "at homes" champagne, claret-cup, and ices are not given. The tea should be made in teapots, instead of in urns, at both large and small "at homes."

At small "at homes" the tea is usually served in the smaller of the two drawing-rooms, or in an adjoining boudoir or ante-room. The tea is then poured out by the young ladies of the house, or by the hostess herself, but seldom by maid-servants when served in the drawing-room.

The most convenient manner, however, of serving tea is to serve it in the dining-room, unless the number of guests is limited, when it would appear unsociable if they were to congregate in the dining-room, leaving the hostess comparatively alone in the drawing-room.

When tea is served in the dining-room, the guests are usually asked by the servant in attendance if they will have tea before being ushered into the drawing-room.

At small teas, the cups of tea should be handed to the ladies by the gentlemen present, or by the young lady officiating at the tea-table, and gentlemen generally stand about the room, or near the tea-table, at small "at homes."

Receiving Guests.—The servant should precede the guests to the drawing-room as in "morning calls."

At large "at homes" the hostess should receive her guests at the drawing-room door, and shake hands with each on arrival. The drawing-room door should remain open, and she should stand within the doorway.

At small teas, the drawing-room door should not remain

open, and the hostess should receive her guests within the room, as at " morning calls."

The guests should arrive from a quarter-past four until half-past five or six o'clock. The guests are not expected to remain the whole three hours specified, and are at liberty to remain as long or as short a time as they please. The earliest arrivals are generally the first to leave.

When the hostess judges it expedient to do so, she introduces one or two of the ladies to each other, either in a formal manner (see Chapter II.), or in a semi-formal manner, by saying, "Mrs. A., I don't think you know Mrs. B."; but she should not say this unless quite certain that Mrs. B. desires the acquaintance of Mrs. A., or that Mrs. A. has no objection to knowing Mrs. B.*

It is rather the exception than the rule to make general introductions on these occasions. Introductions should only be made when the hostess is aware that the persons introduced would be likely to appreciate each other, or for any reason of equal weight.

The guests should go to the tea-room with any gentlemen of their acquaintance present, or in the case of ladies with each other, if they have not done so on arrival.

This move to the tea-room is usually made in the intervals between music, recitations, etc.

Occasionally, the hostess introduces one or two of the gentlemen present to the ladies of highest rank for the purpose of sending them into the tea-room.

A lady should place her empty cup on any table near at hand, unless a gentleman offers to put it down for her. It is optional whether a lady removes her gloves or not, and many prefer not to do so.

At large " at homes," the hostess remains at her post the whole of the time, and hardly ever sits down. At small

---

* See chapter " Conversing with New Acquaintances," in the work entitled " The Art of Conversing."

" at homes," she should move amongst her guests, conversing with them all more or less. When there are daughters, they should assist their mother in entertaining the guests.

When ladies are acquainted, they should take an opportunity of speaking to each other. It is usual for ladies to move about the rooms at afternoon " at homes " to speak to their various friends and acquaintances; and they are by no means obliged to remain seated in one spot unless desirous of doing so.

When music is given at afternoon " at homes," it is usual to listen to the performance, or at least to appear to do so; and if conversation is carried on, it should be in a low tone, so as not to disturb or annoy the performers.

It is not necessary to take leave of the hostess at afternoon " at homes," unless she is standing near the drawing-room door when the guest is passing out, or unless she is a new acquaintance, and the visit a first one at her house, when it would be polite to do so.

When it is late, and but a few guests still remain, these few should make their adieus to the hostess.

At these afternoon teas or " at homes," the hostess should not ring to order the door to be opened for the departing guest or for her carriage to be called, as at " morning calls." The guests make their way to the hall, and the servants in attendance call up the carriages as they are asked for.

Carriages should always be kept in waiting at afternoon "at homes," as ladies are sometimes unable to remain longer than a quarter of an hour.

The guests either remain in the hall or in the dining-room until they hear their carriages announced.

Gratuities should never be offered to servants at these entertainments, or, in fact, at any entertainment whatever.

Afternoon Concerts.—When afternoon concerts are given, invitations should be issued on the usual " at home " cards, which can be purchased with the words "at home," etc., already printed, or they are printed to order, with the name and address of the hostess. The name of the person invited should be written above the name of the hostess at the right-hand corner of the card.

The date under the line "at home" should be in the centre of the card beneath the name of the hostess; the hour should be written at the left-hand corner, and the letters R.S.V.P. The printed address should be at the right-hand corner.

The names of the performers should be added at the bottom of the card at the right-hand corner.

The hour usually fixed for a concert is 3 o'clock.

The hostess should receive her guests at the drawing-room door, when they should at once seat themselves. The seats should be arranged in rows down the centre of the room, and sofas and settees should be placed around the room.

The programme of a concert is divided into two parts, and at the conclusion of the first part the guests should repair to the dining-room for refreshments, which are served as at large "at homes."

Afternoon Dances.—Invitations to afternoon dances should be issued on "at home" cards in the manner already described. "Dancing" should be printed in the corner of cards, and the hour of "4 to 7" o'clock substituted for that of "3" o'clock. The words "afternoon dance" should not be written on an invitation card, and there is no other received form of invitation for afternoon dances than the one already given.

Afternoon dances are very popular at watering-places, military stations, small towns in the vicinity of London, etc., but are seldom given in London itself.

Refreshments should be served during the whole of the afternoon, from 4 to 7, as at large "at homes."

The ladies should remove their jackets or wraps in the cloak-room, but retain their hats or bonnets; the hostess should receive her guests at the drawing-room door, as at an afternoon "at home."

Bridge Teas occupy an important place in social life. They are a convenient form of entertainment, as they allow of a small number of guests being invited, even as few as eight persons being considered a reasonable number of players to invite, while twenty-four is distinctly an outside one. The average number is in most instances sixteen, all told.

The play usually commences at 3.30, sometimes earlier, and continues until 7.30, allowing an interval for "tea" at 4.30.

The invitations to these informal gatherings are either issued in friendly notes or on visiting cards. If on the latter, the words "at home," day, and date are written under the name of the hostess, while "Bridge, 3.30," or "3 o'clock" is put in the corner of the cards opposite the address.

The hostess arranges beforehand the places the guests are to occupy at the different tables; this is done that the good players may play together. When all have arrived, the hostess tells her guests where to sit, and is herself one of the players. On taking their seats they cut for partners. She does not invite guests to look on, as it would necessitate her not playing, but talking to them while they remain; besides conversation is discouraged, as it distracts the attention of the players from the game.

The ladies retain their hats, but remove their coats, furs, etc., on arrival.

CHAPTER XX

An "At Home" day signifies that a lady is at home to her friends and acquaintances on one particular day in the week. She should intimate this fact by printing upon her visiting cards the days on which she is at home. Thus : " Thursdays in March," or " Thursdays in March and April," or any day of the week she thinks proper to name. These cards she should leave in person on those who are not at home when she calls, or they can be sent by post. Those she finds at home she should inform that her " at home " day is " Thursday." She should not leave her visiting card in this case, only two of her husband's cards, and the " at home " day should not be written upon them.

On the " at home " day, calls should be made from three to six, or from four to six. The first comers should leave before the afternoon tea hour and should limit their call according to the degree of intimacy existing, remaining from a quarter of an hour to an hour, as the case may be.

A Hostess or her Daughter should pour out the Tea on these " at home " days when tea is not served in the dining-room as at " at homes," which should be done when the number of visitors is very considerable.

The popularity of a hostess is tested on these " at home " days by the number of visitors who call during the afternoon, and when " at home " days are not a success, socially speaking, she should discontinue them after a certain time, and should substitute an occasional "at home."

It depends not a little on the social standing of the lady who has an "at home" day and upon the locality in which she lives, as to whether the "at home" day is a failure or the reverse. In the outlying districts of town it has its advantages, when to make a call amounts to almost a journey, and when acquaintances are few in the immediate neighbourhood. Again, it has its advantages when ladies are much occupied during the week, and when their time is given up to an engrossing occupation, charitable or artistic, at home or away from home, literary or scientific, at studios, museums and public institutions, etc., work undertaken for their own amusement, profit, or advancement, or for the benefit of others. To these ladies an "at home" day is a convenience. One day in the week is all they can allow themselves apart from their important engagements, and to them quiet privacy and leisure are indispensable. Fashionable ladies consider an "at home" day to be a great tax upon their time and inclinations. Their engagements are too numerous to admit of giving up one whole afternoon in every week on the chance of people calling. Not only long-standing but impromptu engagements preclude this sacrifice. It would be a breach of politeness not to be at home to callers on an "at home" day, and many things might occur to necessitate absence from home on that particular afternoon. If, however, absence is unavoidable, a relative might take the place of the hostess on the "at home" day in question.

The people who thoroughly enjoy "at home" days are those who have more time on their hands than they know what to do with. The few calls they have to make are soon made, the few friends they have to see are soon seen, occupation they have none, and they are grateful for the opportunity "at home" days offer of meeting their friends and finding a hostess at home.

CHAPTER XXI

GENERALLY speaking, etiquette is followed in the colonies and in India by English men and women very much as in the mother country as regards its principles, rules, and observances. One marked difference occurs in the hours of calling, it is true, they being regulated by climate. In hot climates, the early morning hours, before noon, and late evening hours, after sunset, are, according to the fashion of the place, the chosen hours for calling; but in more temperate climes—resembling our own—the afternoon hours are, as with us, the hours for calling. Again, the rule that residents should call upon new-comers, whether they be visitors of other residents or intending residents, holds equally good both in civilian and military circles alike.

In all colonies and dependencies "Government House" is the centre to which all society gravitates—that is to say, that all new-comers, whether they are to become permanent or temporary residents, providing their social position warrants the action, hasten to make known their arrival by writing their names and addresses in the visitors' book kept at each Government House for the purpose. The object of doing this is to be received at Government House, and thus to obtain an entrance into the society of the place. What follows upon this social observance—it hardly merits the name of civility, such calls being actuated by self-interest in the first instance—depends upon a variety of circumstances, the position of the caller, and whether the stay is to be permanent or temporary, whether introductions are brought or not, and so on. The invitations extended to them are regulated accordingly. They may be limited to afternoon " at homes "; or receptions, dinners, and dances may be included ; or a visit to the summer residence of the Governor and his wife may also be reckoned amongst invitations, as this latter is not an unusual display of hospitality accorded to certain individuals.

How the Governor of a Colony should be addressed by his guests depends upon his rank. As he represents the sovereign, it would be quite correct to address him as " Sir," as being the most deferential mode, and Governors as a body rather like to be thus addressed. In the case of a Governor being a knight—a very usual contingency—it would be equally correct to address him as " Sir George," and not as " Sir." When a Governor has not received knighthood, he should be addressed as " Mr. A——," when it is not desired to be too stiff and formal.

In conversation, when referring to the Governor—he being present—it should not be " The Governor," but " Lord Blank," " Sir George," or " Mr. A—— said so and so," unless strangers are present, before whom it would seem right to be a little formal.

In addressing a Governor by letter, the envelope should be directed to " His Excellency Sir George Blank," however friendly its contents may be ; but when writing to a Governor's wife, it has not been thought right to style her " Her Excellency," but simply " Lady Blank," unless in the case of a Viceroy's wife, as in India or Ireland; but as against this the point was raised some years ago, and it was then decided that the wives of Governors were entitled to be so addressed.

Colloquially, the members of a Governor's suite refer to both the Governor and his wife as " His " and " Her

Excellency," and style them "Your Excellency," and all who approach them officially, being of inferior rank, do likewise; but socially they are seldom so addressed.

A Colonial Bishop should not actually be styled "My Lord," or referred to as "The Lord Bishop," if it is desired to be quite correct; but "My Lord" or "The Lord Bishop" is now often used by persons who know it is not the proper style of address, but make use of these titles, wishing to be more deferential than scrupulously correct. In writing to a colonial bishop, the envelope should be addressed to "The Right Rev. the Bishop of ——," and the letter commenced "Right Rev. Sir" or "Dear Bishop Blank."

A colonial officer who has received the King's special permission to retain the title of "Honourable" which he bore in his colony, is accorded at Court, *i.e.* at a levée, Court ball, etc., the same precedence as a peer's son, who is styled "Honourable," but this does not practically give him any rank or precedence at ordinary social gatherings, where that special grant is unknown or ignored. Also the privilege confers no rank or precedence upon the wife or daughters of a colonial Honourable, just as the wife of a Right Honourable here has no special precedence.

The title of Honourable cannot continue to be borne by a retired colonial officer or Legislative Councillor unless it has been specially authorised by the sovereign on the recommendation of the Secretary of State for the Colonies.

CHAPTER XXII

IT is the custom that those who wish to be invited to Government House (Viceregal House) at Simla, or elsewhere, should, immediately on arrival, write their names in the visitors' book kept for that purpose, and they are sure, if in general society, to be asked to one or more of the receptions held during the season. They are introduced to the Vice-Queen—as the wife of the Viceroy is termed—by one of the *aides-de-camp* in waiting.

When a lady is the wife of a Government official, it gives her a position in society in India which perhaps she would not otherwise have, and is in itself a passport to most functions. Official rank is everything in India.

As regards attending the Viceregal Drawing-rooms, they are only held in Calcutta and in the evening. If a lady has been presented at a Court in England, she can attend a Drawing-room in Calcutta ; but, if she has not been presented at home, she must be introduced by some other lady who has been presented at the Viceregal Court.

In writing unofficially to the Governor-General of India, it would not be correct to use the title of "Viceroy," and the proper superscription is "His Excellency The Right Hon."; or, if a Duke, "His Excellency The Duke of ——"; or, if a Marquis, "His Excellency The Most Honble. Marquis of ——," etc.

To the wife of a Viceroy the address should be "Her

Excellency the Duchess of ——," "Her Excellency The
Marchioness of ——," "Her Excellency The Countess of
——"; or "Her Excellency The Lady Blank," if the wife
of a Baron.

When addressing a Viceroy or Vice-Queen colloquially
or unofficially, "Your Excellency" should not be used in
either case. The title only in both instances should be
employed.

On being introduced to either of their Excellencies, it
would be correct to curtsy.

CHAPTER XXIII

GARDEN-PARTIES

GARDEN-PARTIES are entertainments that are annually given. If the weather is fine, the more enjoyable it is for the guests; if wet, a garden-party resolves itself into a large " at home."   In almost every county a series of garden-parties is held by the principal ladies of their respective neighbourhoods during August and September, nothing but absence from home, illness, or some equally good reason being considered sufficient excuse for the non-fulfilment of this social duty.

The county at large expects to be invited at least once a year to roam about in the beautiful park of the lord of the manor, to row on the lake, to play lawn-tennis on the lawn, to wander through the winding paths of the shady, leafy shrubberies, to admire the brilliant hues of the geraniums bedded out on parterre and terrace, or the variegated asters, or the late Gloire-de-Dijon roses, which at the end of August are in their fullest beauty.   Then there are the conservatories through which to saunter, and from which to beat a retreat, if the sun is too powerful, into the mansion itself, the reception-rooms being generally thrown open on the occasion of a garden-party.

A garden-party is an occasion for offering hospitality to a wide range of guests—people whom it would not be convenient to entertain save at this description of gathering. Invitations are on these occasions freely accorded to ladies, from the energetic lady of eighty to the little lady of eight,

One great advantage offered by a garden-party is that it is immaterial to what extent ladies are in the majority, and it is a reproach to a county rather than to a hostess if the muster of guests is eighty ladies against twenty gentlemen.

Invitations to a Garden-party should be issued in the name of the hostess, and within three weeks to a week of the date fixed. "At home" cards should be used for this purpose, and the words "and party" should be invariably added after the names of the invited guests.

"Croquet" or "Tennis" should be printed in one corner of the card, the hour, 3 to 7 o'clock, above, the day and the date beneath the name of hostess. "Weather permitting" is seldom written upon the card, and the guests are expected to arrive even though the afternoon should be showery and overcast, and only a thoroughly wet afternoon, with no break between the showers, should prevent their appearing. In the country, ladies think little of a drive of ten miles to attend a garden-party.

Arrangements for Garden-Parties. — Garden-parties or croquet-parties are given on different scales of expenditure, and the preparations are regulated accordingly.

When a garden-party is given on a small scale, and the preparations are comparatively few, refreshments should be served in the house. (For the usual refreshments provided, and for the general arrangements, see work entitled "Waiting at Table," p. 82.)

A good supply of garden-chairs and seats should be placed on the lawn and about the grounds, rugs spread on the grass for those who sit out, and several sets of croquet provided for players.

At large garden-parties a band is considered a necessary adjunct, and the band of the regiment quartered in the vicinity is usually available for these occasions.

A band gives *éclat* to an out-door gathering and confers local importance upon it. Apart from this, the strains of a band enliven an entertainment of this description in no little degree. The place where the band is stationed is a rallying-point for the company, and the expense and trouble consequent upon engaging a band are repaid by the amusement it affords.

The matter of engaging a military band is generally undertaken by the master of the house, rather than by the mistress, as, in the first place, the consent of the colonel of the regiment has to be obtained as a matter of form and courtesy before the arrangements are completed with the bandmaster.

Conveyance for the band has also to be provided and discussed with the bandmaster, and also refreshments for the bandsmen; and these details are more effectually carried out by a host than by a hostess.

Occasionally a large marquee is erected in which to serve refreshments, but more frequently the refreshments for the general company are served in the house, and only cool drinks dispensed in a tent to the cricketers or lawn-tennis players.

Cricket-matches are often the *räison d'être* of a garden-party, rendering it popular with both ladies and gentlemen. The cricket-match in this case generally takes place in a field near to the grounds of the mansion, the match commencing about twelve o'clock, and the general company arriving about half-past three, or punctually at four, to witness the finish.

Golf now ranks first amongst fashionable outdoor amusements with both sexes. Private links are comparatively few, but club links exist in almost every neighbourhood—ladies' clubs, men's clubs, and clubs for both ladies and gentlemen.

Croquet or tennis tournaments are frequently the occasion

of giving garden-parties, and some very exciting play takes place.

When a tournament is held it takes the form of a garden-party ; it usually lasts two days. The arrangements made for holding it depend upon circumstances, and it takes place, as do archery-matches, in either private or public grounds.

Amusements.—When a number of children are expected at a garden-party, performances of marionettes, or Punch-and-Judy, or conjuring are given for their amusement.

In districts remote from town, these shows are difficult to obtain ; therefore amateur showmen come bravely to the rescue, and their kindly efforts to divert the juveniles meet with due appreciation on all sides.

Not seldom a little amateur music is given at a garden-party—not a pre-arranged programme of music, but impromptu performances. These good-natured efforts to enliven the company occupy about an hour, and such performances take place in either the drawing-room or music-room of the mansion.

Garden-parties seldom terminate with a dance, though occasionally dancing closes the afternoon's amusements.

The time occupied by croquet or tennis precludes all desire on the part of the players for further exertion in the shape of dancing, and young people apparently prefer playing croquet from 3 to 7 on the lawn to dancing in a marquee or in the drawing-room at that hour.

A host and hostess receive their guests at a garden-party on the lawn ; strangers should be introduced to the hostess by those who have undertaken to bring them to her house, and she should shake hands with all comers. It is also usual for guests to shake hands with the hostess on departure, if opportunity offers for so doing.

Garden-parties commence from 3.30 to 4 o'clock, and terminate at 7 o'clock.

In making preparations for a garden-party, stabling for the carriage-horses and motor-cars of the numerous guests should be taken into consideration, and refreshments provided for the men-servants and chauffeurs.

Public afternoon concerts, bazaars, and flower-shows are essentially functions frequented by ladies *en masse*, and it is the exception, rather than the rule, for gentlemen to accompany them; again, at private afternoon gatherings, ladies usually appear unaccompanied by gentlemen.

When a garden-party is a very large function, it is not unusual to put the words "garden-party" on the invitation cards in place of the words "at home"; thus: "The Countess of A—— requests the pleasure of Mr. and Mrs. B——'s company at a garden-party on ——," etc.

CHAPTER XXIV

THE first garden-parties in town are usually given early in June, and continue during this and the ensuing month. The garden-parties at Lambeth Palace and Fulham Palace are the pioneers of the garden-party season, and the lead is followed by general society with more or less alacrity.

Town garden-parties resolve themselves into large receptions held out-of-doors, and those who know what crowded drawing-rooms imply in the sultry days of June are particularly glad of this change of *locale*, and willingly spend an hour or more at one of these out-of-door *réunions*, instead of thinking a quarter of an hour's stay all too long within doors, where it is a case of heat *versus* draught, and difficult to determine where it is the most objectionable, in the drawing-room, tea-room, or on a staircase. Although these functions are designated "garden-parties," yet the real style and title is "at homes," the address being sufficient indication to the invited guests as to the description of entertainment to be given, as the spacious gardens and lawns in and around London where these annual parties are held are well known to society at large. A band playing in the grounds where the garden-party is given would appear to be a *sine quâ non,* but the excellence of the same is merely a question of expense. Thus guests have the pleasure of listening to the strains of splendid bands, and also the disappointment of hearing others far below the average.

As this fickle climate of ours is not to be counted upon for twenty-four hours at a stretch to remain fine, it. is seldom considered advisable to have the whole of the refreshment tables out-of-doors, and thus only ices, strawberries and cream, and ice cups are served out-of-doors; tea, coffee, and the rest, with ices, strawberries and cream, being invariably served within doors.

Refreshment tables out-of-doors considerably take off the strain from the tables in the tea-rooms, especially during the first half-hour, when the great rush is made in this direction. Again, should heavy rain set in, the servants can easily remove pails of ice and bowls of strawberries and cream out of harm's way. Even a large tent or marquee is not considered altogether desirable for refreshments, as under a burning sun the air within becomes over-heated and oppressive, while in the case of a downpour the results are almost disastrous.

The popularity of garden-parties is incontestible in propitious weather. A variety of reasons conduce to this; for one thing, movement is so pleasant an exchange from the almost stationary position guests are compelled to take up in a crowded drawing-room. Again, the number of guests invited is so much greater than to an "at home," that the chance of meeting a corresponding number of friends and acquaintances is trebled; or, on the other hand, if but a few friends should be present among the guests, yet the situation does not amount to isolation and boredom; and the alternative of sitting under a shady tree or sauntering about on the lawns listening to the strains of the band, is positive enjoyment in comparison to sitting in the corner of a drawing-room barricaded by a phalanx of ladies, or standing wedged in the midst of the same. It is small wonder, therefore, that invitations to these outdoor functions are hailed with satisfaction and pleasure.

Arrivals at a garden-party are made almost simultaneously, or if not quite this, they follow in rapid succession, so that host and hostess have a short interval between arrivals and departures; and this offers an opportunity to give more than a shake of the hand to many of the guests, *i.e.* a little friendly conversation; while at an "at home" the hostess has to be at her post from 4 p.m. to 7 p.m., as guests arrive continuously, even close up to the hour named for departure.

The host is expected to be present at a garden-party, and almost always is so; but his presence at his wife's "at home" is left a little doubtful, and his absence is often accounted for on the ground of its being unavoidable; but the trivial reasons that many men advance to their wives for their non-appearance prove how glad they are to escape from the ordeal on any terms. A man in the open air is at his best, and therefore a garden-party appeals to a host almost as much as it does to a guest.

Although the words "at home" are in general use when issuing invitations to these functions, yet occasionally the words "garden-party" are substituted in lieu of them on the "at home" cards, when the gatherings are unusually large; thus: "Viscountess B—— requests the pleasure of Mr. and Mrs. G——'s company at a garden-party on ——," etc.

CHAPTER XXV

The Garden-Party Season has been widened out by the introduction of "Evening Garden-Parties" into the list of country festivities, and this form of entertainment has found great favour with all.

Invitations are issued on the usual "at home" cards, the hours from 9 to 12 p.m. Occasionally "dancing" is printed on the cards, but not often, as it is not usual to combine an evening garden-party with a dance, except when only young girls and young men are invited.

Some little perplexity is felt by the recipients of evening garden-party invitations as to the style of dress that should be worn. Should ladies wear morning dress or evening dress? Men are equally in doubt on this point. Ought they to wear evening dress or not? Although this is not stated on the invitation cards, yet it is tacitly understood that ladies are expected to appear in the usual garden-party attire—smart, pretty dresses and hats or bonnets, and small fashionable wraps carried in place of sunshades in the event of the evening air proving somewhat chilly. Evening dress, when worn at one of these "at homes," looks particularly out of place. The thin evening shoes, which must of necessity be worn with this style of dress, suit neither dewy grass nor stony gravel; and although at the evening concerts at the Botanic Gardens many ladies wear "evening dress" with smart evening cloaks, this is beside the question. They go for a short half-hour or so, not for a three hours' stay. Anyhow, at evening garden-parties, the rule is not to wear evening dress as far as ladies are concerned. Men, on the other hand, one and all, are expected to do so, morning dress being looked upon as out of place on these occasions. A light overcoat is inseparable from evening dress, therefore it is not considered risky wear for men even on the chilliest of summer evenings.

As to the arrangements for one of these evening garden-parties. It is usual to have tea and coffee, and light refreshments during the whole of the evening, from arrival to departure, and to give a light supper a little before twelve o'clock. The gardens and grounds are illuminated with coloured lamps and lanterns, extensively or moderately, as the case may be. A band is considered indispensable, but a good one does not seem to be equally imperative, to judge from the indifferent performances of various bands heard on these summer evenings. However, country audiences are not too critical, knowing that to engage a good band from a distance entails considerable expense, and that evening garden-parties would be singularly few if superior music was insisted upon. Thus the local band is encouraged to do its best, and to allow long intervals to elapse between each selection.

In the case of an evening turning out decidedly wet, guests invited from a distance seldom put in an appearance, while the nearer neighbours do so, and the evening garden-party becomes an evening reception within doors, shorn of its numbers, it is true, but a pleasant gathering, nevertheless, especially with those who know how to make the best of a *contretemps* caused by unpropitious weather.

CHAPTER XXVI

Invitations to Luncheon are very much the order of the day in fashionable society. Those who look back some few years remark the importance now accorded to this mid-day meal, and contrast it with the past. The lateness of the dinner-hour in a measure accounts for the position now taken by luncheon in the day's programme, joined to the fact that it offers another opportunity for social gatherings; and as the prevailing idea seems to be to crowd into one day as much amusement and variety and change as possible, invitations to luncheon have become one of the features of social life.

Invitations to Public Luncheons are not now confined to the celebration of local and civic events, but take a far wider range, and are given on every available opportunity when the occasion can be made to serve for assembling a large party of ladies and gentlemen. Luncheon is by some considered to be rather a lady's meal than not, although in reality invitations are given as frequently to the one sex as to the other. Yet the predominance of ladies at luncheon is due to the fact that the majority of gentlemen are too much occupied at this hour to be at liberty to accept invitations to luncheon, while others, more idle, breakfast at so late an hour that to them a two o'clock luncheon is a farce as far as eating is concerned. Outside of those who are busy men and those who are idle men, and consequently late risers, there is another semi-occupied class of men who are always amenable to an invitation to luncheon.

This institution of luncheon is invaluable to people who have many friends, acquaintances, and relations to entertain, as invitations to this meal are given for every day in the week, with or without ceremony, with long notice or short notice, or on the spur of the moment.

Ladies enjoy the society of their hostess at luncheon far more than at a dinner-party. At the former meal she makes general conversation with her guests on both sides of the table; at the latter she is monopolised by her immediate neighbours, by the gentleman who takes her down to dinner, and by the one who sits at her right hand, while she leaves her guests to be entertained by the gentlemen who take them in to dinner. At luncheon things are different; there is no going in to luncheon, conventionally speaking, save on official and public occasions.

Luncheon occupies a prominent place in the round of hospitalities. Invitations to luncheon are not formally issued on invitation cards, unless some especial reason exists for giving a large luncheon-party, in which case it takes rank as an entertainment.

Large luncheon-parties are given on occasions such as lawn-tennis tournaments and lawn-tennis parties, archery-parties, cricket matches and bazaars, etc.

Semi-official luncheons are given on the occasion of laying the foundation-stone of a church or public building, etc. This class of luncheon is beside the question, as it is rather a banquet than a luncheon, for which printed cards of invitation are issued.

In general society invitations to luncheon are issued by written notes or are verbally given according to circumstances.

Invitations to Luncheon.—A week's notice is the

longest usually given, very little notice being considered requisite.

Many hostesses give their friends *carte blanche* invitations to luncheon; but ladies as a rule seldom avail themselves of this *façon de parler*, as they consider it, and prefer to await a more direct form of invitation. Gentlemen, on the contrary, are expected to avail themselves of this proffered hospitality without ceremony, as the presence of a gentleman visitor at luncheon is considered an acquisition, the reason, perhaps, being that ladies are usually in the majority at luncheon, and also that the unexpected arrival of one or two ladies would call for a greater amount of attention on the part of a hostess seated at luncheon than would the unexpected arrival of gentlemen, ladies requiring especial attention to be shown to them in the matter of a place at table, etc., while gentlemen are ready to offer attention instead of requiring it, and to take any place at table, whether convenient or otherwise.

As a rule, the number of ladies present at luncheon greatly exceeds the number of gentlemen present, unless at a luncheon-party, when a hostess usually endeavours to equalise the numbers as far as possible; but it is not imperative for her to do this, and it is immaterial whether there are as many gentlemen as ladies present at luncheon or not.

Luncheon is a very useful institution to a mistress of a house, as it enables her to show a considerable amount of civility to her friends and acquaintances.

She can invite to luncheon those it might not, for various reasons, be convenient to invite to dinner; as for instance, young ladies, single ladies, elderly ladies, ladies coming to town, or into the neighbourhood for a few days only, and so on.

The usual rule in houses where there are children old enough to do so, is for the children to dine at luncheon with their governess, whether there are guests present or not.

In Town the Usual Hour for Luncheon is 1.30 to 2 o'clock; in the country it is generally half an hour earlier. The guests are expected to arrive within ten minutes of the hour named in the invitation, as although punctuality is not imperative, it is very desirable.

A guest, on his or her arrival at a house, should not, if previously invited, inquire if the mistress of the house is at home, but should say, on the servant opening the door, " Mrs. A. expects me to luncheon."

When the guests are self-invited, they should inquire if the mistress of the house is at home.

Guests are conducted to the drawing-room before luncheon. The servant precedes them, as at morning calls.

When guests arrive after the hour named for luncheon, they should be at once ushered into the dining-room, and their names announced.

When the guests are unacquainted with each other, the hostess should make a sort of general introduction or introductions; that is to say, she should introduce one gentleman to two or three ladies, thus, " Mr. A., Mrs. B., Mrs. C., and Miss D.," making but one introduction in place of three separate introductions, this being the less formal mode of making unimportant introductions.

It is not always possible for a host to be present at luncheon, owing to occupation and engagements, but courtesy to his wife's guests demands his presence when practicable. He should either join them in the drawing-room or in the dining-room, according to his convenience.

Guests are not sent in to luncheon as they are to dinner.

Ladies should not remove their hats at luncheon. They should remove their fur coats and wraps. These should either be left in the hall on arrival or taken off in the drawing-room or dining-room. Short gloves should be removed; elbow gloves may be retained.

Gentlemen should not take their hats with them into the drawing-room, but should leave them in the hall.

Ten minutes is the usual time allowed between the arrival of the guests and serving luncheon, which is usually served at the hour named, the received rule being not to wait for guests.

Going in to Luncheon.

—When the luncheon gong sounds the hostess should say to the lady of highest rank present, "Shall we go in to luncheon?" or some such phrase. (See "The Art of Conversing.") The visitor should then move towards the door. If the host is present, he should walk beside her; if not, the hostess should do so. The other ladies should follow as far as possible according to precedency, the gentlemen going last. Thus the hostess either follows with the ladies or leads the way.

Guests should not go in to luncheon arm-in-arm as at a dinner-party, but singly, each lady by herself, or, when space permits, side by side. Gentlemen likewise, but on arriving in the dining-room, each gentleman should place himself by the side of a lady, or between two ladies, at table.

The hostess should sit at the top of the table and the host at the bottom, as at dinner, but it is immaterial where the guests sit, although as a rule the lady of highest rank sits by the host, and the gentleman of highest rank by the hostess.

A late arrival should, on being ushered into the dining-room, make his or her way to the top of the table to shake hands with the hostess, making some polite excuse for being late.

A hostess should rise from her seat to welcome a lady, but she should not do so to welcome a gentleman.

Luncheon is either served *à la Russe* or not, according to inclination, both ways being in equally good taste, although, as a rule, the joint is served from the *buffet* or side-table, while the *entrées*, game, or poultry are placed on the table.

For further information respecting the arrangements for luncheon, see the work entitled "Waiting at Table."

Formerly it was the custom in some houses for the servants to leave the dining-room as soon as they had helped the various guests to the joint or joints, and handed round the vegetables and the wine, in which case the host and hostess helped the guests to the *entrées* and sweets, or the gentlemen present did so; but now it is invariably the rule for the servants to remain in the room during the whole of luncheon, and to hand the dishes and wine, etc., to the guests as at dinner-parties.

Luncheon usually lasts about half an hour, during which time the hostess should endeavour to render conversation general.

As at dinner, it is the duty of a hostess to give the signal for leaving the room, which she does by attracting the attention of the lady of highest rank present by means of a smile and a bow, rising at the same time from her seat.

The host, or the gentleman nearest the door, should open it for the ladies to pass out.

The ladies should leave the dining-room as far as possible in the order in which they have entered it, the hostess following last.

When the host is not present, the gentlemen should follow the ladies to the drawing-room; but when the host is present, the gentlemen should remain in the dining-room with the host a short time before joining the ladies in the drawing-room.

It is optional on the part of the host whether he returns or not with the gentlemen to the drawing-room, although, if not particularly engaged, it is more courteous to do so.

Coffee is sometimes served after luncheon in the drawing-room. It is handed on a salver immediately after luncheon. The most usual way now, however, is to have coffee brought into the dining-room at the conclusion of luncheon, and handed to the guests on a salver.

N

The guests are not expected to remain longer than twenty minutes after the adjournment to the drawing-room has been made.

Ladies should put on their gloves on their return to the drawing-room after luncheon.

Ladies having carriages should previously desire their coachmen to return for them from three to a quarter-past three o'clock, and the servant should inform each guest of the arrival of her carriage.

When a lady requires a cab, she should ask the hostess's permission to have one called for her.

The subject of leave-taking is fully described in Chapter IV.

CHAPTER XXVII

Breakfast Parties have in certain circles become a feature, and invitations to breakfast are issued both by card and by note.

In official circles breakfast parties are frequently given, the morning hours up to one o'clock being the only disengaged portion of the day, and thus the opportunity is taken for offering and receiving hospitality, and of enjoying the society of friends and acquaintances. The breakfast hour varies from ten to eleven, according to circumstances, and the meal somewhat resembles a luncheon, fish, *entrées*, game, and cold viands being given, with the addition of tea, coffee, and liqueurs.

Punctuality on these occasions is almost imperative, as breakfast cannot be prolonged beyond a given limit, and therefore it is not considered necessary to wait the coming of a late guest.

The guests go in to breakfast as to luncheon. When a party consists of both ladies and gentlemen, the hostess should lead the way with the lady of highest rank, followed by the other ladies, the gentlemen following with the host.

When a party consists of gentlemen only, the host should lead the way with the gentleman of highest rank, and should indicate to the principal of the gentlemen present the places he wishes them to occupy at table; the remainder of the company should seat themselves according to inclination.

The table should be laid as for luncheon, and decorated with flowers and fruit. Tea and coffee should be served from a side table by the servants in attendance.

All dishes should be handed as at luncheon.

For the details of "Breakfast-table Arrangements and Serving Breakfast," see the work entitled "Waiting at Table."

The guests usually leave as soon as breakfast is over, unless the ladies are invited by the hostess to accompany her to the drawing-room, or the gentlemen are invited by the host to smoke a cigarette or cigar previous to their departure.

House Party Breakfasts.—In the country the breakfast hour varies from 9 to 10.30, and in some country houses it is an understood thing that the guests are at liberty to come down to breakfast at any time between nine and half-past ten. In not a few country houses the hostess and the ladies breakfast in their own rooms, and the gentlemen of the party breakfast with the host in the breakfast-room.

The breakfast gong is a signal for assembling in the breakfast-room or dining-room, but it is not the custom to wait for any one beyond five or ten minutes.

The host and hostess at once take their places at the breakfast-table.

When the house-party is a large one, and space permits, a number of small tables should be arranged in the breakfast-room, in addition to a long breakfast-table.

The servants should remain in attendance during breakfast to wait upon the guests.

There is no general move made from the breakfast-table as in the case of luncheon or dinner; the hostess generally remains until the whole of the guests have at least commenced breakfast, save in the case of very late comers, for whom she would not be expected to remain at the head of the breakfast-table.

The guests leave the breakfast-table as soon as they have finished breakfast, without waiting for any intimation from the hostess to do so.

CHAPTER XXVIII

MANY things contribute to draw people into the country and away from town in the month of September; therefore there is a far larger number in each and every neighbourhood inclined for a picnic or a water-party than in the three previous months, June, July, and August.

Picnic parties are sometimes invitation parties, and on other occasions contribution parties, or parties which partake in a measure of the character of both.

Picnics by Motor Car and Picnics by Rail.— Almost every county has its show place, or its ruins, its ruined abbey or its castle, its romantic scenery, and its fine views, its hills or its dales, its waterfalls or its glens. The southern and western counties are as rich in these respects as the eastern counties are barren.

When a picnic party is to proceed to its destination by rail, a saloon carriage is engaged beforehand, and arrangement is made at the nearest hotel to supply the party with luncheon at from 5s. to 10s. per head, according to the style of luncheon required; or hampers of provisions are taken under the charge of one or two men-servants.

If the picnic party proceeds by road, a coach is the favourite mode of conveyance, whether driven by the owner or hired for the occasion. This is a more sociable way of going to a picnic than dividing the party into detachments and conveying them in separate carriages. This is sometimes

unavoidable, and if the party is assembled for a start, it
occasions no little discussion as to how the party should
be divided and conveyed in the various carriages, and it
takes no little tact to arrange this in a satisfactory manner—
to overrule objections, and to make things work smoothly.
Again, the members of a picnic party occasionally find their
way to the place of rendezvous independently of each other ;
but, although this plan saves trouble, it does not promote
sociability, and parties of four or six are apt to clique
together during the day, instead of making themselves generally agreeable. The provision question is a very important
one, and the heads of a picnic party should arrange in
concert what each is to bring in the way of fish, flesh, fowl,
fruit, and wine.

The services of one or two men-servants at a large
picnic party are generally required to arrange the table, to
open the wine, and last, but not least, to collect and repack
the articles used in the way of plate, china, or glass.

A picnic luncheon in September is not always the
al fresco spread under the greenwood tree that it is in July,
and oftener than not is held in the best parlour of a rustic
inn, or, by permission, in a barn or shed, when the weather
is not favourable for camping out.

Usually, when a large picnic party is arranged and got
up by some three or four ladies and gentlemen, they divide
the expenses of the entertainment between themselves, and
determine how many shall be invited, each having the
privilege of inviting a certain number. Other picnics are
got up on a different system, each person contributing a
share towards the general expenses; but these gatherings
are not so sociable as are the invitation picnics.

Invitation picnics where everything is done *en prince*
are extremely enjoyable and friendly affairs ; they are
big luncheons, given out-of-doors instead of indoors, at a
distance instead of at home. But even these are not more

pleasant than those well-arranged little picnics given by officers in country quarters, when the regimental coach conveys a favoured few to some favourite spot.

Water-Parties.—There are many ways of arranging a water-party at yachting stations and at all riverside places. At yachting stations, for instance, a sailing yacht is hired to convey a party of from eighteen to twenty-five to some point of interest on the coast, in which case luncheon and tea are provided at an hotel in the vicinity of the place where the party have landed, and the expenses are equally divided. Not unfrequently, on the return journey, the yacht is becalmed, and does not reach its destination until between two and three the following morning. If it happens to be a fine moonlight night, this prolongation of a water-party is an additional source of enjoyment; but if there is no moon as well as no wind, and the calm betokens a storm, it is the reverse of pleasant. But these little *contretemps*, when they do occur, rather lend a zest to the day's pleasure, and are something to talk about afterwards.

Water-parties are often given by owners of yachts. These are invitation parties, and luncheon, tea, and sometimes dinner, are served on board, and the party land and stroll about, but return to the yacht to be entertained.

Picnic and water-parties in general include as many gentlemen as ladies, whether they are invitation or contribution parties, although sometimes a majority of ladies is unavoidable. Ryde is a favourite station for water-parties, as the island itself, as well as the opposite coast, offer innumerable points of interest for picnicing, and many are able to combine the pleasures of the yacht with those of the steam-launch in one and the same water-party; thus a party sails from Ryde to Yarmouth, Isle of Wight, and then proceeds in a steam-launch to Alum Bay. Steam-launch parties are immensely popular, both on the river and on the coast, and parties are given by the owners of steam-launches, or a steam-launch can be hired by the day. Some picnic on board, and others on shore, as they feel disposed. When, however, a steam-launch is hired for the day, a good look-out should be kept upon the engineer, or he will insist on landing at the most undesirable spots.

Canoe-parties on coast and river are also popular with both ladies and gentlemen, and here again the steam-launch is brought into requisition to convey the party home, as an hour and a half to two hours is an average time to paddle a canoe; after that time the party land either on the rocks or on the shore, and light a fire and boil the kettle for tea. If the tea-drinking and the after-tea ramble are unduly prolonged there is a chance, if on the coast, of the steam-launch running out of coal, and of the party having to return home in their own canoes considerably later than was expected, and not a little fatigued.

CHAPTER XXIX

Juvenile Parties form a prominent feature in the entertainments given during the winter months. There is scarcely a household the children of which are not indulged with one large party at least, while others are allowed as many as two or three children's parties during the winter months. These parties offer no little elasticity as to their arrangement, varying from a child's tea party, composed, perhaps, of five or six children, to a juvenile ball, or fancy dress ball. Some mothers object, on principle, to the latter entertainments, on the ground that to give a large juvenile ball provokes a corresponding number of invitations, and that a round of such gaieties is not good for young children, either from a moral or from a hygienic point of view. Morally, that such amusements are likely to destroy or impair the freshness of childhood, and to engender artificial ideas in their young minds in place of such as are natural and healthy, and that the imitation of the manners and bearing of their elders causes them to become miniature men and women, and divests them of the attributes of artless and unaffected childhood.

The dresses worn by children at these entertainments are of so elaborate a character—and so much pride is exhibited when wearing them—that a spirit of vanity and a love of dress are aroused at a prematurely early age. From a physical point of view, late hours, heated rooms, rich dainties, and constant excitement have a pernicious effect upon children.

There is, of course, an opposite view taken by those who uphold juvenile balls; they consider that children are the better for associating with others of their own age outside of their own family circle, and that in the case of only children such association is calculated to render them lively and intelligent. Another argument in favour of these juvenile parties is, that children who are in the habit of constantly attending them acquire self-possessed and confident manners, and that all shyness, *mauvaise honte* and *gaucherie*, which distinguish many children when in the company of strangers, are dispelled by frequent intercourse with children of all ages. Thus, in place of the noisy game of romps, the little gentlemen ask the little ladies to dance, pull costume bon-bons with their favourite partners, and offer them similar attentions throughout the evening. Of course, there are shy little gentlemen and shy little ladies even at a juvenile ball; but it is the constant endeavour of those who accompany them, whether mammas, elder sisters, young aunts, or grown-up cousins, to persuade them to get the better of this diffidence, and to induce taciturn Master Tommy to dance with timid Miss Tiny. Sometimes Master Tommy is obstinate, as well as taciturn, and his "won't" is as strong as his will. As with all things, so with children's parties, the medium course is, perhaps, the wisest to take, running into neither extreme—avoiding too much seclusion or overmuch gaiety, and rendering such gaiety and amusement suitable to the ages of the children invited. When an evening's entertainment consists of a series of amusements, it is a mistake to crowd too great a variety into the space of four hours, the usual limits of a child's party, for if so the programme has to be hurriedly gone through, and is hardly finished before the hour of departure. No little judgment is required when organising juvenile parties. The hours usually selected for children's parties, whether on a large or small scale, are from four to eight, five to nine, six to ten, or from seven to eleven.

The children on their arrival are received in the drawing-room. In most cases their relatives, either mothers or grown-up sisters, are asked to accompany them.

There is great punctuality observed as regards the hour of arrival, and tea is usually served in the dining-room about half an hour after that named on the invitation card. The interim is generally passed by children in watching each fresh arrival, and in greeting their little acquaintances, comparing notes with each other as to the teas and the parties they are going to, or in amusing themselves with the toys belonging to the children of the house, which are usually arranged on tables for this purpose; and mechanical toys, walking and talking birds, etc., musical toys, picture-books, and dolls, and the latest and newest inventions in the way of playthings afford the little visitors an opportunity for becoming at ease with each other.

Tea is generally dispensed at one end of a long table, and coffee at the opposite end. The governess usually pours out the tea, and one of the daughters of the house the coffee; or failing her, the head nurse or lady's maid does so. Dishes of pound, plum, and sponge cake are placed the length of the table, interspersed with plates of thin bread-and-butter, biscuits, and preserves; either the ladies of the family or the servants in attendance hand them to the children.

When the relatives accompany the children tea is usually served to them in another room, but frequently they do not arrive until tea is over, and the nurses accompany the children to the house.

Amusements.—The arrangements for the evening's amusement are regulated in a measure by the amount of accommodation a house affords, premising that boisterous games are not allowed in drawing-rooms, unless all valuable ornaments or things likely to be broken are removed from the rooms.

If conjuring is one of the amusements provided, it generally takes place in the drawing-room immediately after tea, and lasts about an hour. A dancing-cloth is put down over the drawing-room carpet; rout seats or cane chairs are arranged in rows. The youngest children are seated in the first row. Performing birds, performing dogs, or performing monkeys are also favourite amusements at these parties, and rank next to conjuring in the estimation of children. Punch and Judy or marionettes are popular drawing-room amusements, and either occupies the space of an hour.

When a magic-lantern, or panoramic views, is the entertainment provided, it takes place in the dining-room or library, or perhaps in the housekeeper's room, if large enough for the purpose.

Dancing or games usually precede these amusements, and lasts from half to three-quarters of an hour; little girls dance with each other polkas, valses, and quadrilles, as little girls are, as a rule, more partial to dancing than are little boys, although they one and all, great and small, join with glee in a country dance, or in the Tempête, or in "Sir Roger de Coverley."

Not longer than an hour is devoted to dancing, and this is usually followed by games.

Impromptu charades is a favourite pastime with children; but to avoid the juvenile audience becoming weary and impatient during the preparation of the charades it is as well they should be amused with some quiet game, such as "forfeits," "cross questions and crooked answers," "proverbs," etc. At Christmas and New Year's parties the distribution of presents is a very important feature; Christmas trees are now rather discarded in favour of greater novelties. "Father Christmas," "Santa Claus,"

"The Fairy Godmother," "The Fairies' Well," or the "Lucky Bag" and "The Magic Log," are some of the many devices for the distribution of presents; these popular characters are represented by grown-up persons, and provoke much wonder and admiration amongst children. The presents are usually given at the close of the evening.

Light Refreshments are provided in the dining-room —lemonade, wine and water, every description of cake, sandwiches, crystallized fruits, French plums, figs, almonds and raisins, oranges, etc. Bon-bons containing paper caps, etc., which afford children much amusement, are usually provided.

When a juvenile ball is given a supper is provided; otherwise light refreshments are considered sufficient, and are served twice during the evening. Sometimes the children of the family, if old enough and clever enough, act a little play—some nursery fairy tale, condensed into one act, such as "Beauty and the Beast," "Cinderella," etc.—which lasts about an hour, and is followed by dancing.

When a juvenile fancy ball is given, one or two fancy quadrilles are arranged beforehand, to be danced by the children in costume, the Nursery Rhyme Singing Quadrille being a very popular one.

CHAPTER XXX

Writing Letters of Invitation, and answering letters of invitation, often occupy far longer time in the composition than the writers would care to confess. The difficulty does not lie in an invitation itself or in accepting or refusing it, but rather in the form in which either should be couched, the words that should be chosen, and the expressions that should be used; one person is afraid of being too *empressé*, another of being too formal or too stiff; one is fearful of saying too little, another of saying too much.

When invitations are issued on dinner cards or on "at home" cards, the note of acceptance should be as brief as is the printed card of invitation, and to the printed card requesting the pleasure of Mrs. Blank's company at dinner, the stereotyped answer is invariably Mrs. Blank has much pleasure in accepting Mrs. Dash's kind invitation for Saturday the 21st, or Mrs. Blank regrets that a previous engagement will prevent her having the pleasure of accepting Mrs. Dash's kind invitation for Saturday, the 21st.

As regards those invitations that refer to visits of some days' duration, those accustomed to give this description of entertainment, know exactly what to say and how to say it. The conventional civilities or affectionate cordialities, as the case may be, occur in their proper places; but one point is made clear in either case, namely, the length of the visit to be paid. There are people who are under the impression that to specify the exact length of a visit is in a degree inhospitable, and not sufficiently polite; and they, therefore, as a sort of compromise, use the ambiguous term "a few days" in lieu of distinctly defining the limit of these invitations. So far from vague invitations such as these being an advantage to invited guests, they not seldom place them at a disadvantage at more points than one. They are uncertain on what day they are to take their departure. They do not wish by leaving a day earlier to disarrange any little plans that their hostess may have contemplated for their amusement; neither do they wish to prolong their visit a day later, lest by so doing they should break in upon any engagements that she may have formed on her own account independently of her visitors. It is also not a little awkward for guests to tell their hostess that they think of leaving on Thursday by 12.20 train. It might have suited the hostess very much better that her visitors should have left on the Wednesday, and in her own mind she had perhaps intended that the visit should end on that day; but, having left the invitation open, more or less, by saying "a few days," there is nothing left for her but to sacrifice her own arrangements to the convenience of her guests, as without discourtesy she could hardly suggest to them that they should leave a day earlier than the one they had named, and the visitors remain unconscious of having in any way trespassed upon the good nature of their hostess.

"A few days" is also an unsatisfactory wording of an invitation to visitors themselves; as a rule, it means three or four days, but there is also an uncertainty as to whether the fourth day should be taken or not. Those who interpret "a few days" to mean three days, make their plans for departure accordingly; failing this, they are compelled to leave their plans open, and stay from three to five days, according as chance and circumstances may dictate. A lady would perhaps require a little addition to her wardrobe in the matter of a five days' visit over that of a three days' stay; but this is a trifling detail, although it helps to swell the list of minor inconveniences which are the result of vague invitations. There are, of course, exceptions to every rule, and there are people who use this phrase of "Will you come and see us for a few days?" in the *bonâ fide* sense of the word, and to whom it is immaterial whether their guests remain three days or six days; but such an elastic invitation as this is usually given to a relative, or to a very intimate friend, whose footing in the house is that of a relation, and with whom the hostess does not stand on ceremony, as far as her own engagements are concerned; and people on these friendly terms can talk over their departure with their hostess, and consult her about it without the faintest embarrassment.

The most satisfactory invitation is certainly the one that mentions the day of arrival and the day of departure. Thus, after the *raison d'être* of the invitation has been stated, the why and the wherefore of its being given follows the gist of the letter : " We hope you will come to us on Wednesday the 23rd, and remain until the 27th." It is, of course, open to a hostess to ask her visitors to prolong their stay beyond the date named if she sees reason for so doing ; but this is the exception rather than the rule in the case of short visits, and guests take their departure as a matter of course on the day named in the invitation. Hostess and guests are perfectly at ease upon the subject, and guests do not feel on delicate ground with their hostess, or fear to outstay their welcome. When a visit has been paid it is polite, if not imperative, to write to the hostess and express the pleasure that has been derived from it. Oftener than not some little matter arises which necessitates a note being written apart from this ; but whether or not, good feeling and good taste would dictate that some such note should be written, and, as it can always include little matters of general interest in connection with the past visit, it need neither be over ceremonious nor coldly polite.

To write a letter asking for an invitation, or to
answer a letter asking for an invitation, is in either case
a difficult letter to write, as many have ere this discovered.
When a married lady asks for an invitation for a young relative or friend staying with her, to some dance or "at home"
to which she herself is invited, the note is simple enough,
and the answer is generally a card of invitation or a written
permission to bring her. Again, in the case of asking for
invitations for gentlemen, if a lady is going to a ball, she
can without hesitation, ask for cards of invitation for one or
two gentlemen friends of her own, mentioning their names
in the note. In this case also the answer is generally in the
affirmative, as men are always acquisitions at a ball. The
awkwardness of the situation arises when a good-natured
person is solicited to obtain an invitation to a smart ball for
a lady and her daughters, or for the young ladies only, the
latter knowing some one who would chaperon them if they
could only get an invitation. If the lady who asks for the
invitation is a fashionable ball-giver, the probability is that
her request will be granted; but if the contrary, the reverse
will most likely be the case. Even when writing to an
intimate friend, there is always a delicacy in asking for an
invitation for a third person, and society appears to become,
year after year, still more exclusive on this point. Many
people are reluctant, or decline altogether, to put themselves under an obligation of this nature, even for those
with whom they are most intimate; it may be that the
number of refusals good-natured people have received from
their friends when trying to render services of this description, have made them chary of putting themselves forward
again in a similar manner: it is chilling to be told that
the list is over full, or that so many people have been
refused already, or that there is not a card to spare. But a
few years ago a ball was not considered a success unless
it was an over-crowded one; the popularity of the ball-
giver was shown by the guests scarcely being able to find

standing-room.   Thus, invitations were given right and left to the friends of those who asked for them.

But the fashion of to-day is to style a crowded ball-room a "bear-garden," and to confine the invitations, with but very few exceptions, to those who are strictly on the visiting list of the ball-giver; and pretty girls may sigh in vain for an invitation to a ball given even by a relative or acquaintance of their own, if not on their visiting list.   Still, invitations are constantly asked for by people for their friends, and sometimes they are given and sometimes they are refused, as the case may be, but much depends upon the position of the one who solicits the favour.

If the giver of an entertainment wishes to oblige the petitioner, she will stretch a point to do so; if not, she will write a polite note of excuse, giving one of the reasons before mentioned.   It is thoroughly understood people do not ask for invitations for themselves, whatever they may do for their friends, and that they would not do so unless they were themselves invited.   Living at a distance modifies, however, this latter rule; and friends in the country often ask for invitations for friends in town, and *vice versâ*.

Dinner invitations are, as a matter of course, never asked for; but invitations to garden-parties, afternoon "at homes," and afternoon teas, are frequently asked for and readily given.   Some are intimate enough at the house where they visit to take a relative or friend with them to these afternoon gatherings without observing the punctiliousness of asking for an invitation; others, on less intimate terms, do not venture upon doing so.

In all cases when an invitation is asked for, a hostess should never neglect to send a reply, and should not take for granted that her friends will naturally understand that silence gives consent, for under the circumstances it is very possible to interpret it to signify a refusal.

CHAPTER XXXI

MANY reasons exist for declining invitations other than the plea of a prior engagement.

" Mrs. M. regrets ('much regrets,' or 'very much regrets') that a previous engagement prevents her having the pleasure of accepting Mrs. N.'s 'invitation,' or 'kind invitation.'" When on more intimate terms, Mrs. M. should write in the first person when declining an invitation. It is an open question whether the nature of the engagement should be stated or not. Even intimate friends often confine themselves to the statement of the bare fact only that a prior engagement exists ; others, on the contrary, state the nature of the engagement, and there is no doubt that this latter course considerably softens a refusal and lessens the disappointment experienced, and therefore, when practicable, should always be followed.

When a prior engagement cannot be made the basis of a refusal, then the refusal must rest on other lines; ill health, a severe cold, etc., are valid excuses. Failing these, the refusal should be as follows :—" Mrs. Z. regrets she is unable to accept Mrs. X.'s kind invitation, etc."

It occasionally happens that it is desirable to break an engagement, circumstances having changed the aspect of things. The invitation, perhaps, was a verbal one, and a refusal was not easy at the moment.

Again, impromptu invitations are sometimes refused, having been too hastily accepted—the servant who brought the note waited for an answer, and on the impulse of the moment an affirmative answer was given; the wife had not time to consult her husband, and accepted for him as well as for herself; or perhaps some potent domestic reason that could not be explained induced a subsequent refusal.

The fashionable world accepts refusals as a matter of course, and fills up the gaps with other invitations.

Refusals of dinner invitations from those for whom a dinner party was partly originated are always disappointing, even to the most popular of dinner givers, in the same way that the absence of the principal neighbour from a county entertainment is felt to cast a shadow over the proceedings of the day.

Although printed cards of acceptance and of refusal are in general use, yet many cases arise which render written refusals imperative.

As regards the refusal of invitations asked for, such requests should not be made unless on very safe ground, and with a certainty of meeting with acquiescence, yet occasionally these requests are either unwelcome or inadmissible, and refusals are consequently given; but, unless worded with tact and good nature, they are often the cause of strained relations between both friends and acquaintances.

CHAPTER XXXII

WALKING, DRIVING, AND RIDING

The Usual Hours for Walking in the Park are from 9 until 10.30 a.m. The hours for afternoon walking and sitting in the Park are from 4 to 7 p.m. during the summer months.

The fashionable hours for walking in the Park on Sunday are from 1 to 2 p.m., both in winter and summer; and from 5 to 7 p.m. in the summer months.

Married ladies can, if they please, walk out unaccompanied or unattended in places of public resort in town or on the parades of fashionable watering-places; but married ladies, especially if they are young, usually prefer the society of another lady, not so much, perhaps, for propriety as for companionship, as to walk alone, either in town or at fashionable watering-places, renders a lady more or less conspicuous, especially if she is attractive and well dressed.

A young lady can now also walk by herself in the Park for the purpose of joining her friends and acquaintances, both in the morning and in the afternoon, but she should not sit alone.

Again, young ladies may walk alone in the fashionable streets, but they should not loiter when alone at shop-windows as they pass, but walk at a quick pace from shop to shop, or from street to street.

In the quiet neighbourhoods of towns, suburban towns, and watering-places, young ladies walk unaccompanied and unattended to visit their friends residing in the near vicinity of their homes, or to attend classes, or for the purpose of shopping, etc.   Indeed, great independence is generally accorded in this respect, the line being drawn at evening hours—that is to say, at walking alone after dusk.

At watering-places, and at all public promenades, it is usual for gentlemen to join ladies with whom they are acquainted, and to walk with them for a short time when it is apparent that their company is desired, but not otherwise.

Ladies and gentlemen, whether related or not, should never walk arm-in-arm, unless the lady is an elderly one, or an invalid, and requires this support.

Driving.—From 3 to 6.30 are the received hours for the afternoon drive during the summer, and from 2.30 to 4.30 during the winter.

The following rules as regards entering and leaving a carriage apply to a motor-car or an electric brougham as far as the construction, make, and size of the same render it possible.

When driving in an open or close carriage or motor-car it is quite immaterial whether the owner occupies the right-hand or the left-hand seat.   The seat she occupies depends upon which side she enters, as the lady driving with her should enter before her and should seat herself on the furthest seat.

A visitor should always enter the motor-car or carriage before the hostess.

When three ladies enter a motor-car or carriage the young unmarried lady should take the back seat and the two married ladies should occupy the front seat ; this is a matter of courtesy on the part of a young lady due to married ladies and not strictly demanded by etiquette.

A husband should sit with his back to the horses, or by

the side of the chauffeur in the case of a motor-car, when a lady is driving with his wife.

A gentleman should be the first to get out of a motor-car or carriage, with a view to assisting the ladies to do so.

As a rule the hostess should leave the carriage or car after her guest and not before her, unless it is more convenient to do otherwise.

When a lady is merely calling for an acquaintance to take her for a drive, she should not descend from her car or carriage for the purpose of allowing her to enter it before her.

In the afternoon young ladies may drive alone in the public thoroughfares, unaccompanied by married ladies. It is permissible for a young lady to drive alone in the Park or in the streets. A married lady can, as a matter of course, drive unaccompanied.

It would be unconventional were a lady to drive alone with a gentleman in his motor-car, unless he were nearly related to her, or unless she were engaged to be married to him.

It is usual for the owner of a carriage to sit with her face to the horses; when a married lady is driving with her she should sit beside her. When young ladies are driving with her in addition to the married lady they should sit with their backs to the horses.

When a lady is driving with her husband, and a young lady accompanies her, she should not offer the front seat to the young lady, but should retain it herself, and even should the offer be made, a young lady should not avail herself of it.

Riding.—As regards riding in town, the hours for practice in the Row are from 8 to 10 a.m. in summer and 9 to 11 a.m. in winter, for inexperienced riders and beginners; young ladies ride with a riding-master or with a riding-mistress, or with a relative, as the case may be.

The hours for riding in the Park range from 9.30 to 10.30 a.m.

It is thoroughly understood that a lady may ride in the Park alone—that is, unaccompanied or unattended—for the purpose of joining her friends. It is argued, in these days of woman's emancipation, that no possible harm or annoyance can arise from the fact of a lady riding unattended, beyond the always possible chance of an accident.

Although great latitude is now allowed to young ladies with regard to riding alone, many parents still prefer that their daughters should be attended by their grooms.

Two ladies frequently ride together, unaccompanied by a gentleman and unattended by a groom.

CHAPTER XXXIII

BOWING

As regards the recognition of friends or acquaintances, it is the privilege of a lady to take the initiative, by being the first to bow. A gentleman should not raise his hat to a lady until she has accorded him this mark of recognition, although the act of bowing is a simultaneous action on the part of both lady and gentleman, as a lady would hardly bestow a bow upon a gentleman not prepared to return it.

The bow between intimate acquaintances takes the character, when given by a lady, of a familiar nod in place of a stiff bow.

When a gentleman returns the bow of a lady he should do so by distinctly taking his hat off and as quickly replacing it, not merely raising it slightly, as formerly, and if he is an intimate acquaintance or friend, he should act in a similar manner.

In France and on the Continent generally, the rule of bowing is reversed, and the gentleman is the first to bow to the lady, instead of the lady to the gentleman.

Between ladies but slightly acquainted, the one of highest rank should be the first to bow to the other; between ladies of equal rank it is immaterial which of the two bows first.

A lady should not bow to persons only known to her by sight, although she may frequently have seen them in the company of her friends.

A lady should bow to a gentleman, either a friend or acquaintance, even when he is walking with either a lady or gentleman, with whom she is unacquainted.

Gentlemen do not raise their hats in recognition of each other, but simply nod, when not walking with ladies, save when a vast difference exists in rank or age.

When a gentleman meets another—a friend of his— walking with a lady or ladies, with whom he himself is unacquainted, he should raise his hat and look straight before him, not at the lady or ladies.

A lady should not bow to another who, being a stranger to her, has addressed a few remarks to her at an afternoon party, as the fact of meeting at the house of a mutual friend does not constitute an acquaintanceship, and does not authorise a future bowing acquaintance.

Ladies, as a rule, are not too ready to bow to those whom they have merely conversed with in a casual way. In the first place, they are not quite certain of being remembered, and nothing is more disconcerting and disagreeable than to bow to a person who does not return it through forgetfulness of the one who has given it, or through shortsightedness, or through actual intention. Short-sighted people are always offending in the matter of not bowing, and almost every third person, comparatively speaking, complains of being more or less short-sighted; thus it behoves ladies to discover for themselves the strength and length of sight possessed by their new acquaintances, or the chances are that their bow may never be returned, or they may continue to labour under the impression that they have received a cut direct; thus many pleasant acquaintances are lost through this misapprehension, and many erroneous impressions created.

A bowing acquaintance is a difficult and tiresome one to maintain for any length of time, when opportunities do not arise for increasing it. The irksomeness of keeping **it**

up is principally experienced by persons meeting day after day in the Park or on public promenades, riding, driving, or walking, more especially when it is tacitly understood that the acquaintance should not develop into a further acquaintance.

It would be considered discourteous to discontinue a bowing acquaintance which has once been commenced.

To know a gentleman by sight through having frequently seen him at balls and parties, does not give a lady the right to bow to him, even though she may have stood beside him for some twenty minutes or so on a crowded staircase, and may have received some slight civility from him.

A lady who has received a little service from a stranger would gladly acknowledge it at any subsequent meeting by a pleasant bow, but as bowing to a gentleman argues an acquaintance with him, and as in such cases as these an acquaintance does not exist, etiquette provides no compromise in the matter. Therefore, if a young lady takes her own line, and rather than appear ungracious bows to a gentleman who has not been introduced to her either directly or indirectly, it is a breach of etiquette on her part; and as to do an unconventional thing is not desirable, the innumerable little services which ladies receive in general society are not further acknowledged beyond the thanks expressed at the moment of their being received.

Bows vary materially : there is the friendly bow, the distant bow, the ceremonious bow, the deferential bow, the familiar bow, the reluctant bow, and so on, according to the feelings that actuate individuals in their intercourse with each other.

When a bowing acquaintance only exists between ladies and gentlemen, and they meet perhaps two or three times during the day, and are not sufficiently intimate to speak, they do not usually bow more than once, when thus meeting in park or promenade.

CHAPTER XXXIV

THE COCKADE

Cockades are worn by servants in livery of officers in the army and navy; of those who hold His Majesty's commissions in the militia and volunteer forces, of lords-lieutenants and deputy-lieutenants.

Retainers of the Crown are entitled to the use of the cockade as a badge of the reigning dynasty.

The fact that cockades are now so frequently worn by men-servants may be accounted for thus :

Deputy-lieutenants are far more numerous now than was formerly the case; almost every country gentleman is a deputy-lieutenant, and consequently his servants are entitled to the use of the cockade. The privilege of appearing in uniform at levées instead of in Court dress has been and is an incentive to many to seek for and obtain the appointment of deputy-lieutenant. Again, all justices of the peace claim the use of the cockade as being "Civil retainers of the Crown"; and although there is no clearly defined rule on this head, according to the late Sir Albert Woods, Garter-King-at-Arms, it has long been tacitly conceded to them.

The custom of livery servants wearing cockades dates from the commencement of the eighteenth century, and was at first purely a military distinction.

The cockade worn by the servants of the members of the Royal Family, and by all who claim to be of Royal descent, is slightly different in shape from that known as the badge of the reigning dynasty, *i.e.* the Hanoverian badge, and is round in shape and without a fan. The military cockade is of an oval shape, terminating in a fan. The civil cockade is of an oval shape also, but without the fan. The naval cockade is identical with the civil cockade.

The white cockade is the badge of the House of Stuart. The black cockade that of the House of Hanover. The servants of foreign ambassadors wear cockades in colour according to their nationalities. Black and white for Germany; black and yellow for Austria; the tricolour for France; scarlet for Spain; blue and white for Portugal; and black and yellow for Belgium.

The word cockade, according to a well-known authority, was borrowed from the French *cocarde*, having originally been applied to the plumes of cock's feathers worn by Croatian soldiers serving in the French army. Some such plume, or in its place a bunch of ribbons, came to be used in pinning up the flaps of the hat into a cocked position, and thus gradually the word passed for the name of the "cocked" hat itself.

CHAPTER XXXV

COUNTRY-HOUSE VISITS

SEPTEMBER is actually the commencement of the country visiting season, the few visits that are paid in August are but a prelude to the programme that is to follow during the succeeding five months.

The visitors received in August are principally relatives. The exceptions to the August family parties are the August cricket parties in the counties where cricket is made a great feature during that month, where the cricket weeks and consequent large country-house parties are of annual recurrence, and where balls and private theatricals form part of the week's amusement. It often follows that people visit at the same houses year after year, they arrange their tour of visits with regard to those invitations which they annually receive ; new acquaintances and new houses whereat to visit are added to the list from time to time and take the place of those which, as a matter of course, drop out of it. Sometimes the invitations fit into each other admirably, like the pieces of a puzzle ; at others there is an awkward interval of a day, or two or three days, to be filled up between leaving one house and arriving at another. If the hostess is, in either case, a relation or an intimate friend, this difficulty is easily surmounted by staying on at one house until the day fixed for arrival at another, or *vice versâ ;* but if a guest is on ceremony with her hostess, or if, as is often the case, new arrivals are expected for the following week, the alternative is to spend a few days in town, as although the house where the next visit to be paid might be within twenty or thirty miles of the house the visitor is about to leave, it would be unusual to spend the interval at an hotel in the adjacent town, as to do so might reflect upon the hospitality of the hostess. On the other hand, invitations are sometimes given independently of dates, but this friendly style of invitation is not given when a large party is invited, and it is understood to mean that the hostess may be quite alone, or may have guests staying with her, as the case may be. This form of invitation is frequently given to people visiting in Scotland, on account of the great distance from town.

It is a very general custom to give shooting parties the first week in September, harvest permitting. If the harvest is late on account of unfavourable weather the shooting parties are postponed until the second or third week in the month; if not, the guests, or at least the crack guns, are usually invited for August 31st, to be in readiness for the morning of the First.

There are large shooting parties and small shooting parties, shooting parties to which royalty is invited and shooting parties restricted to intimate friends or relations, but in either case the period is the same, three days' shooting.

If a party is limited to five guns, seven ladies is the average number invited, the hostess relying upon a neighbour or a neighbour's son to equalise the balance at the dinner-table. The success of house-parties mainly depends upon people knowing each other, or fraternising when they are introduced or have made each other's acquaintance. The ladies of a country-house party are expected, as a rule, to amuse themselves, more or less, during the day. After luncheon there is usually a drive to a neighbouring town, a little shopping to be done there, or a call to be paid in the neighbourhood by some of the party, notably the married ladies, the young ladies being left to their own resources.

At the close of a visit game is offered to those of the shooters to whom it is known that it will be acceptable.

The head gamekeeper is usually instructed to put up a couple of brace of pheasants and a hare. But in some houses even this custom is not followed, and the whole of the game killed, with the exception of what is required for the house, finds its way into the market, both the local market and the London market.

The first three weeks of September gives a hostess little anxiety on the score of finding amusement for the ladies of the party, as so many aids out of doors are at her command at this season of the year. This is a great advantage, as although some few ladies possessing great strength of nerve have taken up shooting as an amusement and pastime and acquit themselves surprisingly well in this manly sport, yet ladies in general are not inclined for so dangerous a game, and even those intrepid ladies who have learnt how to use their little gun would never be permitted to make one or two of a big shooting party, even were they so inclined.

The hostess and the ladies of the party invariably join the shooters at luncheon, and even some of the ladies go out with the shooters in the morning to watch their prowess in the field ; but this entails a great deal of walking where partridge shooting is concerned, which is quite another thing to covert shooting in November and December.

A good hostess has great opportunities for distinguishing herself when entertaining a country-house party, from the arrival of the first carriage to the departure of the last. Her consideration and tact are so successfully exerted that somehow her guests always find themselves doing exactly

P

what they like best and in company with those who are
most congenial to them, to say nothing of the comfort of
the general domestic arrangements, which seem to have
been arranged exclusively for their convenience. If they
wish to drive, there is a carriage or motor-car at their disposal; if they prefer a constitutional, there is some one very
agreeable desirous of walking with them. The daily papers
are always to be found, the post-bag goes out at a most
convenient hour by the hand of a special messenger, the
dinner is of the best, and the evening is of the cheeriest.
Bridge as a rule is played in most houses, and several tables
are arranged in the drawing-room to accommodate the
would-be players.

Occasionally, when the birds are wild and sport is slack,
a sort of picnic luncheon is held in the vicinity of a keeper's
lodge, under the shade of some wide-spreading trees, when
the ladies join the party; but in September keen sportsmen
rather despise this playing at shooting, and resent the inter-
ruption caused by the company of ladies at luncheon, and
prefer to take it in the rough and smoke the while. Every
day of the week is not thus given up to shooting, and there
are few owners of manors who would care to provide five
days' consecutive sport for their guests, and two days' hard
shooting is probably followed by what is called an idle day.
On these off days in September the hostess often gives a
garden-party, or takes her guests to one given by a neighbour at some few miles distant; or she holds a stall at a
bazaar and persuades her guests to assist her in disposing of
her stock; or she induces her party to accompany her to
some flower-show in which she takes a local interest; or the
host and one or two of the best shots start early after breakfast to shoot with a neighbour, and the remainder of the
guests drive over to a picturesque ruin, where they picnic,
and return home in time for the eight-o'clock dinner. If the
owner of a mansion has a coach the whole party is conveyed
on it, otherwise the motor-cars are brought into requisition,

while saddle horses are provided for those who care to ride. A country-house party occasionally resolves itself into two or more cliques, as far as the ladies are concerned; gentlemen, as a rule, are not much given to this sort of thing. On the first evening, as soon as the ladies have left the dining-room for the drawing-room, these little cliques are tacitly formed, and continue unbroken until the close of the visit. There are many reasons which call these cliques into existence—old intimacies revived, new acquaintanceships to be strengthened, unwelcome acquaintanceships to be avoided, and so on. These cliques are by no means agreeable to the hostess, indeed, quite the contrary—but she is powerless to prevent their being formed, and she is herself sometimes drawn into one or other of them, and sometimes altogether excluded from them. Any one who is at all conversant with country-house visiting is aware how thoroughly the influence of the clique pervades the atmosphere of the drawing-room; and yet, perhaps, at country-house parties more friendships are formed and intimacies cemented than at any other gatherings.

The evening amusements at country-house parties vary very much according to the proclivities of the hostess or those of her daughters. At some houses dancing is the order of things for a couple of hours or so after dinner, but this mode of spending the evening does not always commend itself to the gentlemen, who, after a long day's walking through wet turnips and over heavy ploughed land, or a hard day's riding over stiff fences, rather incline towards the *dolce far niente* of a luxurious armchair than to the pleasures of the mazy valse, and are proportionately grateful to a hostess who does not call upon them to undergo any further exercise than what they have already gone through for their own pleasure.

In most country-house parties bridge forms the chief if not the only amusement, and is played not only after dinner but in the afternoon also. Amateur theatricals, and *tableaux vivants*, impromptu charades, dumb crambo, thought reading, and feats of nerve power, etc., are fashionable amusements and easy of accomplishment : the former demands considerable study and plenty of time for rehearsal, therefore theatricals are generally engaged in when the party is composed of relatives rather than of acquaintances, and when the visit would be perhaps prolonged to ten days or a fortnight.

Some hostesses prefer keeping late hours to early hours, and do not retire until after twelve ; this does not commend itself to the gentlemen, as they are not supposed to adjourn to the smoking-room until the ladies have left the drawing-room, and gentlemen like to spend a couple of hours in the smoking-room after dinner.

In hunting counties the breakfast is usually an early one, varying from nine o'clock to half-past nine, according to whether the ride to covert is likely to be a long or a short one ; but, as a rule, the nominal breakfast hour is 9.30 o'clock. A certain amount of latitude is allowed to guests as regards coming down to breakfast ; they do not assemble in the morning-room, but all make their way to the breakfast-room, and seat themselves at once at table, while many ladies breakfast in their own rooms.

In Scotland, an invitation to shoot often means a visit of three weeks. The accommodation of the shooting-box or lodge may be limited or primitive, and it is very often both of these ; but it matters very little to the sportsman what sort of bed he sleeps on, or how he is made to rough it, providing the grouse are plentiful. On some of the moors there are but cottages and farmhouses for the occupation of the sportsmen, but on others the houses are excellent, and let with the moors, as many take a moor season after season and invite their friends to shoot between the 12th of August and October. The grand shooting parties that are annually given in Scotland by owners of large estates and fine shootings extends throughout the whole of the shooting season, and guests come and go without intermission; as one leaves another arrives. Certain houses or castles are much gayer than others; to some very few ladies are asked, the majority of the guests being gentlemen—probably the hostess and two ladies and eight men—in others, the numbers are more equal; in others, again, the party sometimes consists entirely of men with a host and no hostess. Ladies generally ask their most intimate friends to Scotland rather than acquaintances, as they are left to themselves the whole of the day, dinner being often postponed until nine o'clock, on account of the late return of the sportsmen.

South of the Tweed, September invitations are usually given for three or four days, from Tuesday till Saturday; married couples, young ladies, and young men, are all asked, and the ladies find amusement in lawn-tennis, or in attending or assisting at some neighbouring bazaar or fancy fair, as in this month county bazaars are very popular, and the visitors at one house lend their services in conjunction with the visitors at another, to hold stalls at a bazaar got up by a third influential lady; and thus the stalls are well stocked, and the fashionable stall-holders give an impetus to the whole affair.

Ladies see very little of the gentlemen between breakfast and dinner. The shooters start about eleven, and seldom return much before seven.

When it is dark at four, those who prefer ladies' society and tea to the smoking-room and billiards, make themselves presentable and join the ladies.

As regards the Etiquette of Visiting at Bachelors' Houses.—It is thoroughly understood that ladies should be accompanied by their husbands, and young ladies by their father and mother, or by a married couple with whom they are on terms of great intimacy, in which case the married lady acts as chaperon to the young ladies. Young ladies cannot stay at the house of a bachelor unless chaperoned by a married lady, or by a female relative of their host. A widow and her daughter could of course join a party of ladies staying at a bachelor's house, or stay on a visit to him were he alone, or entertaining bachelor friends.

When a bachelor gives a country-house party, and nominally does the honours himself, occasionally one of the married ladies of the party tacitly takes the lead.

The position of a young widower is similar to that of a bachelor as regards society. Later in life, the contrary is the case; a widower with grown-up daughters gives entertainments for them, and the eldest daughter does the honours, thus reducing the position again to that of host and hostess.

CHAPTER XXXVI

Ladies in the Hunting-Field.—There is no arena better fitted to display good riding on the part of women than the hunting-field, and no better opportunity for the practice of this delightful accomplishment and for its thorough enjoyment. It is urged, however, that it argues cruelty of disposition and unwomanly feeling to join in the pursuit of a poor, miserable, hunted fox, and worse still to be in at the death, and that women are liable to be carried away by the enthusiasm of the hour to applaud and to witness what they would otherwise shrink from. This argument has a certain weight, and deters many from actually hunting who would otherwise join in the sport, and they make a compromise by regularly attending the meets, and even witnessing a throw-off of a fox-break covert. Every strong point that a rider possesses is brought out in the field. The canter in the Row, the trot through the country-lanes, or the long country ride are very feeble substitutes for the intense enjoyment experienced when taking part in a good run ; the excitement felt and shared in by the whole field exhilarates and stimulates, and renders fatigue a thing out of the question, not to be thought of until the homeward ride is well over.

Considering the number of ladies who hunt, the accidents that occur are surprisingly few, for the obvious reason that ladies do not attempt to hunt unless their skill as good horsewomen is beyond all question. Their husbands, their fathers, their brothers would not allow them to jeopardise their lives, unless their riding and experience, their courage, their nerve, and their instruction justified the attempt.

There are also two other weighty considerations necessary to success—a good mount, and a good lead. The father or husband invariably selects the one, and the friend —either of the fair rider or of the husband or brother— gives the all-important lead, without which few ladies venture upon hunting, save those few who are independent enough to cut out their own work.

Ladies, who are naturally fond of riding, cannot always indulge in the pleasure of hunting, on the ground of expense, for instance. A lady may possess a fairly good horse for ordinary purposes, to ride in the Row, or for country exercise, but very few gentlemen of moderate means can afford to keep hunters for the ladies of their families as well as for themselves, although, in fiction, this is freely done. If a lady has one good hunter of her own, she may expect two days' hunting a week, providing the country is not too stiff, and the meets are fairly convenient. Occasionally, a mount may be obtained from a good-natured friend, whose stud is larger than his requirements ; but this is not to be depended upon in every-day life, and popular ladies and first-rate riders are more in the way of receiving these attentions than the general run of ladies.

As regards the presence of young ladies in the hunting-field, there are two opinions respecting its advisability, apart from the question of whether it is or is not a feminine pursuit. The long ride home in the November and December twilight, in the company of some member of the hunt, who has become the young lady's cavalier for the time being, is not to the taste of many parents ; chaperonage must of necessity be greatly dispensed with in the hunting-field, and this is an objection which many fathers advance against their daughters hunting.

Some husbands entertain equally strict views on this head, and are of opinion that the boldest rider and the best lead to follow in the field is not always the guest they would most desire to see at their own firesides.

Hunt-Breakfasts.—A lady should not go to a hunt-breakfast at the house of a country gentleman if unacquainted with him, or some member of his family, unless asked to do so by a mutual acquaintance. All gentlemen riding to hounds, whether strangers to the host or not, have the privilege of entering any house where a hunt-breakfast is given and accepting the hospitality offered. The breakfast, which is in reality a cold collation, with the addition of wine, liqueurs, ale, etc., is usually laid out in the dining-room, and no ceremony whatever is observed; the gentlemen come and go as they please.

The mistress of the house should either be present at a hunt-breakfast and receive the ladies who arrive in the hall or dining-room, or she should receive them in the drawing-room, where refreshments should be brought to them.

When a hostess intends riding to hounds, she is often mounted before her neighbours arrive, in which case she invites them to enter the house for refreshments, if they care to do so.

Gentlemen who go down into a County for a few days' hunting only seldom wear " pink," and prefer riding to hounds in black coats.

The members of the hunt wear pink as a matter of course, but it is considered better taste for a stranger to wear a black coat than to appear in a *new, very new,* unspecked red one.

Sporting Terms.—Persons unversed in matters appertaining to " country life " and " country sports," town bred, and who have had little or no opportunity of acquiring a knowledge of the subject from personal experience, can hardly fail to commit many and various mistakes when brought into contact with sportsmen and their sports.

A knowledge of sporting matters and sporting terms, and the etiquette observed by sportsmen, is only arrived at by associating with those thoroughly conversant with the subject, and with whom "sport" has formed part of their education so to speak.

The Shooting Season commences on the 12th of August with grouse shooting in the north of England, Scotland, and Ireland. Partridge shooting commences on the 1st of September and terminates on the 1st of February.

The finest partridge shooting is allowed by general consent to be found in the eastern counties.

Partridge driving does not take place until January to any great extent.

Pheasant Shooting commences the 1st of October and terminates the 1st of February.

Hares may be shot up to the 1st of March.

Rabbits may be shot all the year round.

Rooks are shot during the spring and summer.

It is difficult to make a would-be sportsmen comprehend the strict etiquette maintained between the owners of manors; that is to say, he would think nothing of crossing the boundary of his host's manor, "gun in hand," if he felt inclined to follow a bird or hare he had wounded, oblivious of the fact that, in the first place, the greatest punctiliousness is observed between gentlemen in the matter of trespassing on each other's land when out shooting; and, that unless the greatest intimacy existed, a sportsman would hardly venture to pick up his dead bird if it had fallen on a neighbour's manor, and would on no account look for a wounded bird, but for a dead one only. In the second place he would carefully observe the rule of leaving his gun on his own side of the boundary, and would certainly not carry it with him to his neighbour's land. These are points that strangers invited for a few days' shooting very often fall foul of, creating thereby much unpleasantness for their host through their ignorance and inexperience.

When a gentleman is invited to join a shooting-party, it would not be necessary for him to take a loader with him, as his host would find a man to perform that office for him, unless he had a servant with him capable of performing that duty; but if he were residing in the neighbourhood he would, as a matter of course, take his loader with him when asked to join a shooting-party, and in both cases he would shoot with two guns, as to shoot with one gun only causes a vexatious delay, more especially if the one gun should happen to be a muzzle-loader, for nothing is more irritating to a party of sportsmen than to be kept waiting while the one muzzle-loader is being loaded, they themselves using breech-loaders.

Another cause of offence to sportsmen is for a gentleman to be noisy when out shooting, that is to say, to be "loudly talkative," or "boisterously merry," or given to indulge in exclamations when a bird rises, or when a bird is missed; your true sportsman maintains a strict silence.

There are numberless other points relating to field sports wherein the "inexperienced sportsman" is apt to give offence, but which would take up too much space to enter into in a work of this description.

The Fees, or Tips to the Gamekeepers, vary from 10s. to £5, according to the number of days' shooting enjoyed or the extent of the bag.

For one day's partridge-shooting the tip to the head

gamekeeper would be a sovereign; for a good day's pheasant-shooting, as much as two sovereigns would probably be given. A gentleman who does not tip or fee up to this mark is not likely to find himself too well placed in a battue.

The cost of a game licence is £3, and lasts twelve months, from 1st August to the 31st of July the following year, or £2 from the 1st of August to the 31st of October, or £2 from the 1st of November to the 31st of July in the following year, or £1 for fourteen days.

CHAPTER XXXVII

THE etiquette with regard to shaking hands is not an open question, it is distinct enough and simple enough for all exigencies, but yet there is individual temperament to be taken into account which in many drives etiquette out of the field, if by etiquette is understood not merely stiff propriety of action, but politeness in the truest sense of the word, and doing that which is exactly the right thing to do. Etiquette rules when to shake hands and when not to do so, when to bow and when not to bow; but in spite of this knowledge, which is within every one's reach, there are many mistakes made on this head.

For instance, one does not offer to shake hands when expected to do so; another offers to shake hands three times; one displays unwarrantable warmth in shaking hands; another extends two fingers only; one shakes hands in a limp and uncomfortable manner, and takes the extended hand merely to drop it; another literally pumps the extended hand, or crushes the rings into a lady's fingers when shaking hands with her.

A lady who does not shake hands when expected to do so is actuated by one or other of the following reasons —she did not wish to shake hands with a certain acquaintance, and preferred to bow only, or she was not aware whether she should have shaken hands or not.

The gentlemen who shake hands with great warmth and *empressement* are two distinct individuals; the one is

cordial and large-hearted, and has a friendly grasp for
every one—a grasp indicative of kindliness, geniality, and
good fellowship—the other wishes to ingratiate himself in
certain quarters, and loses no opportunity of demonstratively
shaking hands, but no one is deceived by this spurious
imitation of the real thing.

When a lady gives but two fingers to people
whom she does not care about, she is always a person who
fancies herself, and who feels very fine ; she doubtless is, but
her good breeding and her good feeling are both in question
when she takes this method of showing the superiority of
herself and her position over that of other people.

There are other eccentricities indulged in by different
people who shake hands when they should not, and people
who do not shake hands when they should.

It depends upon whom a lady is introduced to, or upon
who is introduced to her, whether she should or should not
shake hands. She should not shake hands on being casually
introduced to a person altogether a stranger to her; but
yet there are so many occasions when it is both proper and
correct to shake hands on being introduced, that the rule
on this head is a very elastic one.

For instance, a host and hostess should shake hands with
every stranger introduced to them at their house.

A lady should shake hands on being introduced to the
relations of her intended husband.

A lady should shake hands on being introduced to the
friend of an intimate friend.

When a lady has entered into conversation to any extent
with some one to whom she has been introduced, and finds
she has much in common with her, she should shake hands
on taking leave ; but if she has only exchanged a few commonplace sentences, a bow would be all that is necessary.

A lady usually takes the initiative with regard to shaking
hands as with bowing ; but in reality it is a spontaneous

movement, made by both lady and gentleman at the same moment, as the hand ought not to be extended or the bow given unless expected and instantaneously reciprocated.

A young lady should not offer to shake hands with one not expectant of the honour.

Shaking hands on taking leave is, with some few people, a graceful and pleasant fashion of saying good-bye; intimate friends hold the hand while the last words are being said. Women hold each other's hands thus on parting, and some few men take each other's hands; but with them it is rather a foreign fashion, and is principally followed by those who have lived much on the Continent; for, as a rule, an Englishman prefers the hearty English shake of the hand.

A lady having once shaken hands with another, should continue to do so at subsequent meetings, unless a coolness of manner warns her that a bow would be more acceptable.

With regard to shaking hands at a dinner-party with acquaintances: if the dinner-party is a small one, and there is time to shake hands, it is correct to do so; but when there is little time before dinner, and no good opportunity for shaking hands, bows to acquaintances at distant parts of the room, or when seated at the dinner-table, are sufficient recognition for the time being.

At an evening-party it depends upon opportunity whether acquaintances shake hands or not.

The fashion of raising the arm when shaking hands is followed by very few in the exaggerated style in which it was first introduced, but a modification of it has distinctly become the fashion in general society.

The hand, instead of being extended straight out, is now offered on a line or parallel with the chest, a trifle higher than the old-fashioned style, and the fingers of the hand are held and gently shaken, but the palm is not grasped or even touched.

CHAPTER XXXVIII

AN unmarried lady, unless she be a maiden-lady of a recognised age and standing, cannot act as an orthodox chaperon; but, on the other hand, a young married lady could do so with the greatest propriety, as could a brother from the age of eighteen; of other relatives it is not necessary to speak.

Young ladies are now frequently asked to dinner-parties without a chaperon, a hostess constituting herself chaperon for the occasion. Dances are also given to which it is understood chaperons are *not* invited, the hostess again acting in that capacity, but at large balls and dances chaperonage is considered indispensable for young ladies. At theatres and evening concerts chaperonage is distinctly required; but at morning concerts and *matinées*, companionship rather than chaperonage is needed.

As regards morning hours. Young ladies may now walk together in the Park and elsewhere; ride together, attend classes together or alone, go to luncheon or afternoon tea alone or together at the houses of friends and acquaintances, quite unaccompanied by a chaperon. They may also visit at country houses without a chaperon, the hostess performing this duty.

At all out-door gatherings, such as garden-parties, tennis-parties, cricket-matches, golf-meetings, etc., the chaperonage required is of the slightest, and for which any might be made available.

CHAPTER XXXIX

PRESENTATIONS AT THE VICEREGAL COURT, DUBLIN
CASTLE

THE Drawing-rooms at Dublin Castle are held by the Lord-
Lieutenant of Ireland and his wife, in St. Patrick's Hall,
at ten o'clock in the evening, instead of in the afternoon,
as at Buckingham Palace.

A Lady who desires a presentation at the Viceregal Court must be presented by a lady who has herself
been presented thereat, and it is necessary that she herself
should be present on the occasion, save under exceptional
circumstances. A lady is not allowed to present more than
three ladies, except officially.

A Lady who proposes being presented at a Viceregal Drawing-room must send to the Chamberlain's office
by five o'clock, three days previous to the Drawing-room,
a card with her name and address both in town and country,
and the name and address of the lady by whom she is to
be presented distinctly written thereon, to be submitted to
the Lord-Lieutenant and his wife for their Excellencies'
approval. Also two Presentation Cards must be obtained
at the Chamberlain's office two days before the Drawing-
room—if they have not previously been sent by post—and
must be filled in with the necessary particulars, and taken
to the Castle on the evening of the Drawing-room, one to be
delivered to the official stationed in the Corridor, and the

Q

other to be handed to the Chamberlain, who will announce the name. It is requested that the names may be very distinctly written upon the cards, that there may be no difficulty in announcing them.

A Lady attending a Viceregal Drawing-room, who has been already presented at the Viceregal Court, must leave at the Chamberlain's office, three days previous to the Drawing-room, a card with her name and address, both in town and country, distinctly written thereon. She must bring with her two similar cards on the evening of the Drawing-room, one to be given to the official in the Corridor, and the other to the Chamberlain, who will announce the name.

A lady on entering the Castle on the evening of a Drawing-room towards ten o'clock, finds the hall lined with soldiers, and repairs at once to the cloak-room to leave wraps, etc., and to have her train dexterously arranged over one arm by a female attendant. She then proceeds up the grand staircase, lined with servants in gorgeous liveries, and enters the Corridor, where one of the Presentation Cards is given up to the official in attendance, and she passes down the Corridor into the Long Drawing-room, where a barrier of wood, enclosing a space, is erected at the end. One of the gentlemen of the Household lifts this barrier at intervals to allow of a certain number passing through to the Throne-room, at the door of which her train is let down and arranged by men-servants. If she is to be "presented," the Chamberlain tells her to take off her right-hand glove, and, if royalty is present, informs her that she must make three bows, and says, "Three bows, please." She gives up her second Presentation Card to him, and he calls out her name, and it is passed along to His Excellency by the gentlemen of the household. The Lord-Lieutenant and his wife stand on a daïs, he standing in front of the Throne, which is a grand chair of State, and on either side

—in what are known as the " Pens "—are grouped the visitors staying at the Castle, those who have the private *entrée*, and the members of the Household. The name of the lady who makes the presentation is also called out. The lady presented advances, the Lord-Lieutenant shakes hands with her, but does not now kiss her on the cheek; she then makes him a bow, and bows to his wife, who bows in return. She then retires back to the door leading into the Long Drawing-room, where her train is replaced over her arm. She then proceeds to St. Patrick's Hall, or to the Picture Gallery.

Ladies who attend the Drawing-room only bow to the Lord-Lieutenant and his wife; he bows to them, but he does not shake hands with them or kiss them. In Ireland men invariably accompany their wives to the Drawing-room, having previously attended the Levée; they pass along the base of the semi-circle, and make their bows at the same time as do the ladies.

When all have been received and have assembled in St. Patrick's Hall, a procession is formed, the Lord-Lieutenant walking first, followed by his wife, whose train is carried by pages. The visitors staying at the Castle follow next, and then the members of the Household, the band stationed in the gallery playing " God Save the King " the while. All those present form up in two lines to make a passage for the procession to pass through, and bow low to His Excellency and his wife as they pass.

A supper is not given, only light refreshments of every description. These refreshments are arranged on long tables on one side of St. Patrick's Hall, and at the lower end, under the gallery, tables are placed for tea, coffee, wine, etc. On the opposite side of the hall red-cushioned seats are placed, and the company promenade in and around the Picture Gallery and St. Patrick's Hall during the remainder of the evening.

Ladies wear full Court dress as at Buckingham Palace, and gentlemen uniform or Court dress.

Levées.—Every nobleman or gentleman who proposes to attend a Levée, and who has not yet been received at the Viceregal Court, must be introduced by a nobleman or gentleman who has himself been previously presented thereat.

A Gentleman who proposes to be presented must send to the Gentleman Usher's office by five o'clock, two or three days before the Levée, a card with his name and address, both in town and country, and the name and address of the gentleman by whom he is to be presented distinctly written thereon, to be submitted for the Lord-Lieutenant's approval. He must also obtain two Presentation Cards from the Gentleman Usher's office, and must take them to the Castle on the day of the Levée, the one to be given to the official in the Corridor, and the other to be handed to the Gentleman Usher, who will announce the name to the Lord-Lieutenant.

Any gentleman who proposes to attend a Levée, having been previously presented, must also take two cards with him to the Castle on the day of the Levée, with his name and address, both in town and country, clearly written thereon, to be given up as before mentioned. Again, a gentleman who, having previously attended the Levée, proposes attending the Drawing-room, is requested to bring with him *one* card, with his name distinctly written upon it, to be left in the Corridor. All those entitled to the private *entrée* at Dublin Castle, and availing themselves of the privilege, are permitted to be accompanied only by their wives and unmarried daughters.

Gentlemen wear Court dress or naval and military uniforms, or the uniforms of Lords-Lieutenants of Counties, or of the Royal Irish Constabulary, etc. The Academical habit cannot be worn except when presenting an address from a university. Foreign orders and decorations cannot be worn at the Court of Dublin by British subjects without special authority under His Majesty's royal licence.

CHAPTER XL

The Art of receiving Guests is a very subtle one, difficult to acquire; but when acquired and thoroughly mastered it confers upon a mistress of a house an enviable reputation—that of being a perfect hostess.

With some this is in-bred, and grace and composure and all the attendant attributes which are to be found in this type of hostess sit naturally upon them; but the individuals so gifted represent the few rather than the many. A far greater section of society has to rely upon experience to teach them this useful accomplishment, while with others time alone can aid them in overcoming natural reserve, and want of confidence in themselves, which stand in the way of their assuming this character with anything like success. Those ladies who are innately thoughtless and careless in this respect, neither time nor experience can mould, and what they are at the commencement of their career, they remain to the end of the chapter—very indifferent hostesses. There are varieties of hostesses, according to individual capabilities, and who are known amongst their friends by these appellations : first ranks the perfect or "charming hostess," either title suits her equally well; next to her comes the "good hostess," she is followed by the one who is "not a good hostess"; and the rear is brought up by the one who is decidedly "a bad hostess." Amongst the salient points which distinguish the perfect or charming hostess are perhaps, foremost, a certain facility of putting each individual guest at ease, conveying that the welcome she accords is a personal if not an especial one. Simultaneously with these agreeable impressions is conveyed a sense of the hostess's genial qualities; her charm of manner, her graciousness and her courteous bearing evincing so plainly that she is entirely mistress of the situation: these qualities insensibly react upon the guests, and evoke a corresponding desire to please on their part.

The perfect hostess possesses yet another advantage, viz. a readiness of speech, a faculty of saying the right thing at the right moment and to the right person, and of identifying herself, so to speak, with the susceptibilities of each of her guests.

The good hostess is essentially what is known as a considerate hostess; she makes up for the brighter qualities in which she is lacking by her extreme consideration for her guests. In the charming hostess this consideration is eclipsed by her more brilliant powers of pleasing, it permeates all she does, while in the good hostess it is her strongest point, and upon which is founded her claim to the name. The lady who bears the undesirable reputation of being "not a good hostess" is not "good" in a variety of ways; she means well and does her utmost to succeed, but by some contrariety of the laws which regulate domestic and social affairs, the results of her efforts are always the reverse of what she would have them be. The lady who is not a good hostess sometimes suffers from shyness and reserve which renders her stiff in manner when she would most desire to be cordial, silent when she would be most loquacious, and awkward when she would be at ease.

As there are many reasons why ladies prove to be good hostesses, so there are many reasons why they prove bad hostesses, selfishness and want of consideration for others contribute to these, as do procrastination and a vague idea of the value of time. Ladies with such faults and weaknesses as these produce very much the same impression upon their guests, although, perhaps, one is a little less culpable than is the other.

The selfish hostess is a bad hostess, because, providing she is amused, she is utterly indifferent as to whether her guests are amused or not, her own pleasure and gratification being of paramount importance. Instead of being in readiness to receive her guests she descends late to the drawing-room to welcome them, and is indifferent as to whether there is any one to greet them or not.

The procrastinating hostess, although she is equally in fault, yet, as she hastens to excuse herself, when lacking in politeness to, or consideration for her guests, her excuses are sometimes admitted; but the selfish hostess, if she deigns to excuse herself, does so with such a palpable show of indifference as to her guests' opinion of her actions, that the excuse is oftener than not an aggravation of the offence. A lady who has no regard for time goes to her room to dress at the moment when she should be descending to the drawing-room; or she remains out driving when she should be returning; or she puts off making some very important arrangement for the comfort or amusement of her guests until it is too late for anything but a makeshift to be thought of, if it has not to be dispensed with altogether. Everything that she does or projects is on the same scale of procrastination; her invitations, her orders and engagements, are one and all effected against time, and neither herself nor her guests gain the value or satisfaction of the hospitality put forth. The bad hostess walks into her drawing-room when many of her guests are assembled, either for a dinner-party or afternoon tea, and shakes hands in an awkward, abashed manner, almost as if she were an unexpected guest instead of the mistress of the house.

The host is not at his ease; he is provoked at having to make excuses for his wife, and the guests are equally constrained.

If the host is of a sarcastic turn of mind, he never refrains from saying something the reverse of amiable to the hostess on her entrance. "My dear," he will perhaps remark, "you are doubtless not aware that we have friends dining with us this evening." This remark renders the guests even more uncomfortable and the hostess less self-possessed, and this is often the prelude to an inharmonious evening, with a host whose brow is clouded and a hostess whose manner is abashed.

The mode of receiving guests is determined by the nature of the entertainment. A welcome accorded to some two or three hundred guests cannot be as personal a one as that offered to some ten to thirty guests.

Whatever disappointment a hostess may feel she should not allow it to appear on the surface, and should not be *distrait* in manner when shaking hands with her guests. At large or small gatherings disappointments follow in the course of events, and very few hostesses can say that they have not experienced this in a larger or smaller degree at each and all of their entertainments.

At a ball or evening-party a hostess should receive her guests at the head of the staircase, and should remain there until the majority, if not all, of the guests have arrived.

As the names of the guests are announced the hostess should shake hands with each, addressing some courteous observation the while, not with a view of inducing them to linger on the staircase, but rather of inviting them to enter the ball-room to make way for other guests.

At a ball given at a country house the hostess should stand at the door of the ball-room and receive her guests. When the guests have duly arrived, a hostess at a country-house ball or country-house theatricals should exert herself to see that all her guests are amused. If she sees that the young ladies are not dancing she should endeavour to find them partners. In town she is not required to do this. If the chaperons have apparently no one to talk to she should introduce one of her own relatives, if she cannot give much of her own attention to them, and she should arrange that all her guests are taken in to supper.

At large afternoon "at homes" the hostess receives her guests at the open door of the drawing-room, and has little more time to bestow upon each than at a ball or an "at home." At small afternoon "at homes" she should receive them in the drawing-room, and should rise and shake hands with each arrival.

A hostess should receive her dinner guests in the drawing-room, and should shake hands with each in the order of arrival. She occasionally finds it a trying ordeal to sustain conversation between the arrival of dinner guests and the dinner being served; sometimes this is prolonged for three-quarters of an hour through the non-appearance of a guest who must be waited for. A hostess should, although she knows that her dinner is spoilt by being thus kept back, endeavour to make the time pass as pleasantly as possible, by rendering the conversation general and by making the guests acquainted with each other. The hostess who can tide over these awkward occurrences so that the postponement of dinner from half to three-quarters of an hour is hardly perceived, proves herself to be entitled to be considered a good hostess.

CHAPTER XLI

Ladies are frequently solicited to allow their names to be placed on the lists of lady patronesses of charity balls. A ball committee is desirous of obtaining a list of influential names to lend *éclat* and prestige to the ball, and a charity ball often numbers amongst its lady patronesses the names of many of the leading members of the nobility, followed by those of the wives of the leading county gentry, or by the principal residents of a watering-place or county town ; but it is understood, as a rule, that the duty of giving vouchers or tickets for a charity ball is undertaken by those ladies who are more directly interested in it, whose husbands are on the committee, who make a point of annually attending it, and thus are principally concerned in keeping it select; and although in many counties and in many towns lady patronesses, members of the nobility, do attend, yet it not unfrequently happens that out of a long list of great ladies only three or four are present at a ball.

The members of the leading nobility and gentry of a neighbourhood invariably lend their names to local charity balls, and head the list of patrons and patronesses, but beyond lending their names, and in some cases sending a subscription of money towards the funds of the charity, or a present of game towards the supper, they have very little to do with the ball itself, which is practically in the hands of the local stewards. The exceptions to this rule are the charity balls held in town during the season, such as the Royal Caledonian Ball, the Yorkshire, the Wiltshire, and the Somersetshire Societies' Balls. On these occasions many of the great ladies give vouchers and attend the balls.

When ladies consent to become lady patronesses of a ball, they usually notify to the committee whether they will or will not undertake the duty of giving vouchers or tickets, as the case may be. Some ball committees arrange that vouchers are to be given by lady patronesses, to be subsequently exchanged for tickets, signed and filled in with the name of the person to whom the ticket is given. The lady patronesses in this case receive the money charged for the tickets, and forward it to the committee after the ball, with any tickets that they may not have disposed of.

The ladies who exert themselves to sell tickets are generally those who possess a large acquaintance, whose husbands are members of clubs; therefore, if any person ought to be tabooed for some good social reason, the lady patronesses reap the benefit of their husbands' knowledge, and are thus able to give a polite refusal when tickets are applied for for persons who are not altogether desirable.

It is no doubt a difficult and delicate task for the lady patronesses of a large ball to keep it thoroughly select, and if not very particular respecting those for whom tickets are granted, a ball, though a full one, is likely to prove a very mixed affair, if not somewhat objectionable, by reason of the presence of persons to whom tickets should never have been granted, !on moral if not on social grounds; and though the funds of a charity may gain considerably by the increase of numbers, through a general willingness on the part of the committee or the lady patronesses to grant tickets to every one who may apply for them, yet such policy is very short-sighted, and is seldom practised by those who possess any practical knowledge in the matter, as it is fatal to the reputation of a ball if persons who are objectionable are present at it.

In the case of a ticket being applied for for a person of doubtful antecedents, a lady patroness's best course is to refer the applicant to the ball committee for tickets or vouchers.

Persons not well received in society, or who have ostracised themselves, have a predilection for public balls, and make every effort to obtain tickets of admission; and in some cases, when a refusal has been pronounced by the committee of a ball, the committee has been threatened with legal proceedings.

Unmarried ladies seldom or ever act as lady patronesses, it not being considered advisable to place the discretion of granting tickets in their hands, lest their ignorance of the world should be taken advantage of.

The lady patronesses of a charity ball who undertake to give vouchers or to sell tickets, usually exert themselves to the utmost in inducing as many of their friends as possible to attend the ball.

It depends upon the committee of a charity ball whether tickets are presented or not to the lady patronesses and stewards; but if the funds of the charity are not at a very low ebb, this is generally done in recognition of their services.

The responsibilities of lady patronesses of private subscription balls are light in comparison with those of public charity balls, as persons who attend subscription balls are usually on the visiting lists of one or other of the lady patronesses, while with regard to county balls, lady patronesses are not usually concerned in the disposal of the tickets.

CHAPTER XLII

The Various Periods of Mourning for relatives have within the last few years been materially shortened, and the change generally accepted ; but as some still prefer to adhere to the longest periods prescribed by custom, in the present chapter both periods are given, and it entirely depends upon individual feeling and circumstances which of the two periods is observed.

The time-honoured custom of wearing crape has greatly declined, and with the exception of widows, many do not wear it at all, while others wear it as a trimming only.

A slighter change has also taken place in favour of half-mourning colours, which are now more worn than black and white during the half-mourning period.

Court Mourning when enjoined is imperative, the orders respecting which are minutely given from the Lord Chamberlain's office and published in the official *Gazette ;* but these orders only apply to persons connected with the Court, or to persons attending Drawing-rooms, Levées, Courts, State balls, State concerts, etc.

When the order for general mourning is given on the death of any member of the Royal Family, the order applies to all, although it is optional whether the general public comply with it or not.

The Longest Period for a Widow's Mourning is two years. The shorter period is eighteen months.

Formerly crape was worn for one year and nine months; for the first twelve months the dress was entirely covered with crape. The newer fashion in widows' mourning is to wear crape as a trimming only, and to discontinue its wear after six or eight months, while some few widows do not wear it at all during their mourning, it being optional wear.

Half-Mourning in the longer period commences after a year and nine months, and is worn for three months. In the shorter period half-mourning may commence after fifteen months, and be continued for three months.

The period for wearing the widow's cap and veil is a year and a day. The veil may be *crepé lisse* or *chiffon* in place of crape. It is now the fashion for young widows to wear the cap as a head-dress only, while others do not wear it at all.

Lawn cuffs and collars are worn during the first year, or for six months only, or not at all. After the first year white neckbands and white strings to the bonnet may be worn. Also hats in place of bonnets. Further touches of white may follow during the next three months.

After a year gold ornaments may be worn; diamonds earlier.

Widowers should wear mourning for one year; they usually enter society after three months.

For a Parent the period of mourning is twelve months; ten months black, two months half-mourning, or eight months black and four months half-mourning. The black may be relieved with touches of white after three months. Crape is optional; many prefer not to wear it at all, others as a trimming.

Diamonds—earrings, brooches, etc.—before gold, at the end of three months.

For a Son or Daughter the period of mourning is identical with the foregoing.

For very Young Children or Infants the mourning is frequently shortened by half this period, or even to three months.

For a Stepmother.—The period of mourning depends upon whether the stepdaughters reside at home or not, or whether their father has been long married, or whether their father's second wife has filled the place of mother to them, in which case the period of mourning would be for twelve months, otherwise the period is six months—four months black relieved with touches of white after two months, followed by two months half-mourning.

For a Brother or Sister the longest period of mourning is six months, the shortest period four months.

During the longest period, viz. six months, black should be worn for five months, with a little white after two months, half-mourning for one month. After one month diamonds, pins, and brooches, etc.; gold after two months.

During the shortest period, viz. four months, black should be worn for two months, half-mourning two months.

For a Sister-in-law or a Brother-in-law the period of mourning was formerly the same as for a brother or sister, but the four months' period is now the one usually chosen.

For a Grandparent the longest period of mourning is six months, the shortest four months.

During the longest period black should be worn for three months, relieved with white after six weeks, half-mourning for three months; diamonds after one month, gold after six weeks or two months.

During the shortest period black should be worn for two months, half-mourning for two months.

The custom of wearing crape may now be said to have gone out of fashion as regards etiquette, black being considered adequate mourning, save in the case of widows.

The former crape periods were six months for parents and children, three months for brothers and sisters, three months for grandparents.

For an Uncle or Aunt the longest period of mourning is three months, the shortest period six weeks.

During the longest period black (no crape) should be worn for two months, half-mourning one month.

During the shortest period black for three weeks, half-mourning for three weeks; diamonds after three weeks.

For a Nephew or Niece the periods of mourning are identical with the foregoing.

For an Uncle or Aunt by Marriage the period is six weeks black, or three weeks black and three weeks half-mourning.

For a Great Uncle or Aunt the longest period is two months, the shortest one month.

During the longest period black for one month, half-mourning for one month.

During the shortest period black for one month.

For a First Cousin the longest period is six weeks, the shortest one month.

During the longest period black for three weeks, half-mourning for three weeks.

During the shortest period black for one month.

R

For a Second Cousin three weeks black. Mourning for a second cousin is not obligatory, but quite optional, and often not worn.

For a Husband's Relations the periods of mourning chosen are invariably the shorter ones.

For a Daughter-in-law or Son-in-law the periods are now shortened to six months; four months black and two months half-mourning, or three months black and three months half-mourning.

For the Parents of a Son-in-law or Daughter-in-law the period is one month, black.

For the Parents of a First Wife a second wife should wear mourning for one month, black relieved with white.

For a Brother or Sister of a First Wife a second wife should wear mourning for three weeks, but this is not obligatory, and depends upon the intimacy existing between the two families.

Much Latitude is allowed to Men with regard to the foregoing periods of mourning.

A Hat-band should be worn during the whole of each period, but it is not imperative to wear suits of black longer than half the periods given, save in the case of widowers.

Servants' Mourning.—It is customary to give servants mourning on the death of the head of the house, which should be worn during the period the members of the family are in mourning. Mourning given to servants on the death of a son or daughter is quite an optional matter.

Seclusion from Society.—The question as to how soon persons in mourning should or should not re-enter society is in some measure an open one, and is also influenced by the rules that govern the actual period of mourning adopted.

A Widow is not expected to enter into Society under three months, and during that time she should neither accept invitations nor issue them. Her visiting should be confined to her relations and intimate friends. After three months she should commence gradually to enter into society, but balls and dances should be avoided during the first year.

For a Daughter mourning for a Parent the period of seclusion is six weeks as far as general society is concerned; but invitations to balls and dances should not be accepted until after six months.

For a Parent mourning for a Son or Daughter the period of seclusion is the same as is that of a daughter for a parent.

For a Brother or Sister the period of seclusion is three weeks.

For Grandparents the period of seclusion is from a fortnight to three weeks.

For an Uncle or Aunt the period is a fortnight to three weeks.

For all Other Periods of Mourning seclusion from society is not considered requisite.

When Persons in Mourning intend entering again into society, they should leave cards on their friends and acquaintances as an intimation that they are equal to paying and receiving calls.

When Cards of Inquiry have been left, viz. visiting cards with " To inquire after Mrs. A——" written on the top on right-hand corner of the cards, they should be returned by cards with "Thanks for kind inquiries" written upon them (see Chapter III.).

Until this intimation has been given, society does not venture to intrude upon the seclusion of those in mourning.

Relations and intimate friends are exempt from this received rule.

Funerals.—When a death occurs in a family, as soon as the day and hour for the funeral are fixed, a member of the family should write to those relatives and friends it is desired should follow, and should ask them to attend, unless the date, time, and place of the funeral, and the train by which to travel to the cemetery, are mentioned in the newspaper, together with the announcement of the death.

It is a Mistake to suppose that Friends will offer to attend a funeral, even if they are aware of the date fixed, as they are naturally in doubt as to whether the mourners are to include the members of the family only, or whether friends are to be included also.

In the Country, when a Doctor has attended a family for some years, it is usual to invite him to attend the funeral of one of its members. In town this is seldom done, unless a medical man is the intimate friend of the family.

In the country the clergyman of the parish reads the funeral service, but in town, when the funeral takes place at Kensal Green, Brookwood Cemetery, or elsewhere, a friend of the family is usually asked to officiate ; in which case it is necessary to make an early application at the office of the cemetery for the use of the chapel at a particular hour.

It is customary for Ladies to attend the funeral of a relative if disposed to do so, in which case they wear their usual mourning attire, and follow in their own carriages.

The Doctor's Certificate as to the cause of death is of primary importance, and should be obtained at the earliest possible moment.

Memorial Cards should not be sent on the death of a relative, being quite out of date as regards fashion and custom.

Wreaths and Crosses of white flowers are very generally sent by relatives and friends to a house of mourning the day of the funeral, unless "No flowers, by request" follows the announcement of the death.

When the funeral takes place before two o'clock, the friends should be invited to luncheon. When it takes place in the afternoon, they should be asked to return to the house for tea or light refreshment.

CHAPTER XLIII

ENGAGED

IT greatly depends upon the views held by parents as to the freedom of action accorded to a daughter during her engagement. Some entertain the strictest ideas on this head, and strenuously put them in force.

By "strict ideas" is meant that an engaged couple, except in the presence of a chaperon, are never, under any circumstances, permitted to enjoy a *tête-à-tête*, sit together, walk together, ride together, or meet during any part of the day.

Wisdom and common-sense dictate a middle course of action for the consideration of parents, neither granting too much nor withholding too much.

The length of an engagement determines in most instances the degree of latitude allowed. If it is to last two months, or even less, it is usual to permit the engaged couple to be much in each other's society. The circumstances under which this is accomplished depend upon the position of the parents; if wealthy, and a country house is part of their possessions, the young lady's father should invite the gentleman engaged to his daughter on a visit, or one or two visits, during the engagement.

Or the mother of the bridegroom-elect should invite her future daughter-in-law to stay with her for ten days or a fortnight.

Etiquette prescribes that a young lady must be chaperoned by one of her near relatives at all public places of amusement.

If an engaged couple move in the same set, they meet frequently at the houses of mutual friends ; they are sent in to dinner together when dining out.

To dance with each other at a ball, or dance more than three or four times in succession, and when not dancing to sit out in tea-rooms and conservatories, renders an engaged couple conspicuous, and this is precisely what many mothers are most anxious that their daughters should avoid being, and would rather that they were over-prudent than that they should run the gauntlet of general criticism.

The usual course for engaged couples to take is to go as little into society as possible during their engagement, and to make the engagement as brief as circumstances will permit. If from various causes it must of necessity be a long one, the only alternative for an engaged couple is to render themselves as little conspicuous in general society as a mutual understanding will permit.

When an engagement is first announced, if the families are not previously acquainted, the father, mother, and relatives of the bridegroom-elect should call on the father and mother of the bride-elect at an early date, to make the acquaintance of the bride and her family, and they should write to the bride-elect expressing their approval of the engagement.

The calls should be returned and the letters answered with the least possible delay.

The engagement should be announced to relatives and intimate friends by the mother of the engaged young lady, and if the announcement is to appear in the papers it should be sent by her.

The bride should ask the sisters and cousins of the bridegroom to act as bridesmaids in conjunction with her own sisters and cousins.

When an engagement is broken off, all letters and presents should be returned on both sides.

All wedding presents received by the bride-elect should be likewise returned to the donors.

The mother of the bride should announce to all whom it may concern, the fact that the engagement is at an end.

CHAPTER XLIV

THE German custom of celebrating Silver Weddings has become thoroughly recognised in this country. It is an interesting custom to celebrate the first twenty-five years of married life under the poetic title of a Silver Wedding, but those who can do so must be for many reasons the few, rather than the many; Royal personages, and distinguished and prominent ones for instance, and again, those in humbler walks of life "far from the madd'ing crowd," are also inclined to do so; but the "crowd" that divides them, formed of different classes and different sets in society, will hardly avail itself of the opportunity of celebrating this period of married life. Husbands as a rule dislike the fuss and parade and prominency it entails, and wives are disinclined to announce to their friends and acquaintances that they have been married five and twenty years, and are consequently not so young as they were.

The entertainments given to celebrate a Silver Wedding are : An afternoon reception and a dinner-party. A dinner-party followed by an evening-party. A dinner-party followed by a dance. Or a dinner-party only, of some twenty or thirty covers.

The invitations are issued on "at home" cards some three weeks beforehand, the cards being printed in silver, and the words " Mr. and Mrs. White at home, To celebrate their Silver Wedding " printed on them, with day and date, etc. The dinner cards should also be printed in silver, with the words " Mr. and Mrs. White request the pleasure of Mr. and Mrs. Black's company at dinner to celebrate their Silver Wedding," etc.

For a dance the invitations should be worded " Mr. and Mrs. White at home, To celebrate their Silver Wedding." " Dancing " printed in the corner of the card.

Each person invited is expected to send a present in silver, costly or trifling as the case may be, whether the invitation is accepted or not. These presents should be exhibited in the drawing-room on the day of the Silver Wedding with a card attached to each bearing the name of the giver.

At the afternoon reception the husband and wife receive the congratulations of their friends as they arrive. They enter the tea-room together almost immediately afterwards followed by those guests who have arrived. Refreshments are served as at an afternoon wedding tea. (See page 143.) A large wedding-cake is placed in the centre of the table, and the wife makes the first cut in it as a bride would do. The health of the husband and wife is then proposed by one of the guests, drunk in champagne, and responded to by the husband.

At the dinner-party the husband and wife go in to dinner together, followed by their guests, who are sent in according to precedency. The health of the husband and wife is proposed at dessert and responded to. A wedding-cake occupies a prominent place on the table, and the dinner-table decorations consist of white flowers interspersed with silver.

At the Silver Wedding dance, the husband and wife dance the first dance together, and subsequently lead the way into the supper-room arm-in-arm, and later on their health is proposed by the principal guest present.

The wife should wear white and silver, or grey and silver.

In the country, when a Silver Wedding is celebrated, the festivities sometimes range over three days, but this only in the case of prominent and wealthy people ; balls, dinners, and school-treats being given, in which the neighbours, tenants, villagers and servants take part.

Golden Weddings.—The celebration of a Golden Wedding is rather an English custom, and one that from circumstances can be but seldom observed. It denotes that fifty years of married life have passed over the heads of husband and wife, and is a solemn rather than a festive epoch. Presents on this occasion are not so generally given, and children and grandchildren rather than acquaintances make up the circle of those who offer congratulations.

CHAPTER XLV

Subscription dances are now an established fact, but whether they will ever really become a rival to the dance proper remains to be seen; yet as they supply a want felt, and are recognised by society, the arrangements necessary for carrying them out should be duly noted.

During the winter months they are a feature in certain sets: Subscription dances, private Subscription dances and public Subscription dances, the latter got up for charitable purposes.

The moderate expenses incurred by giving private Subscription dances commend them to many, and there are other reasons to account for their popularity. They are without pretension to being considered smart or exclusive, and are essentially small and early dances. Fashionable ball-goers are not expected to attend them. They commence at 9 o'clock and terminate at 12, light refreshments in lieu of supper are provided, as at an afternoon "at home." (See p. 153.) A piano band is considered sufficient for the purpose, and floral decorations are scarcely ever attempted. The invitations are issued on "at home" cards, with the words "Subscription Dance" printed in one corner.

Subscription dances are sometimes invitation dances and sometimes not. Tickets for these dances are charged for singly or by the series as the case may be. A certain number of ladies form a committee and agree to give a certain number of dances, and the expenses are either borne by the ladies themselves or covered by the sale of the tickets. If invitation dances, a certain number of invitations are allotted to each lady. When otherwise, the ladies dispose of the tickets among their friends. These dances are usually held in a mansion hired for the purpose, and there are several available in different parts of the West End, where spacious rooms can be hired on very moderate terms; in some instances a piano, seats, and other accessories are also included.

Public Subscription dances are held in public rooms or Town Halls, and vouchers are given by ladies on the committee previous to tickets being granted.

The same etiquette holds good at Subscription dances as at other public dances. The early hour at which these dances take place recommends them to some and altogether renders them impossible to others, notably to those who dine late, and who are not inclined to dance at nine o'clock or even at ten o'clock, and who rather resent the frugal style of refreshments offered, and consider that a champagne supper is an indispensable adjunct to a dance.

It should be remembered that Subscription dances were first originated for the amusement of very young people, and it was never expected that they would compete with the fashionable small dances of the day; their popularity was a surprise, and if ball-goers are disposed to hold them in contempt there are others less fashionable and less wealthy who find them very much to their taste.

The great difficulty, however, that ladies have to contend with is the fact that very few men can be induced to attend them, and that those who do accept invitations or purchase tickets are very young men, who have their way to make in the world, and are as yet on the lower rungs of the ladder, and as young ladies are very much in the majority at these Subscription dances, to dance with partners younger than themselves is an almost inevitable result for those who are no longer in their teens.

CHAPTER XLVI

As regards presents in general it should be understood that a present demands a note of thanks in all cases when the thanks cannot be verbally expressed. The notes to slight acquaintances should be written in the third person. To friends, in the first person. This applies equally to presents of game, poultry, fruit, or flowers. Some few people entertain the erroneous idea that presents of this nature do not require thanks. This is not only ungracious but raises a doubt in the mind of the giver as to whether the present sent has been duly received.

Wedding Presents.—When an engagement has been duly announced to relatives and friends, and it is understood that it is to be a short one, wedding presents may be sent until the day before the wedding-day, and the earlier they are sent the more convenient it is for the bride, as she is expected to write a note of thanks to each giver. In each case a letter should be sent with the present expressing the congratulations and best wishes of the donor, and, if possible, a card with the name of the giver should be attached to it for identification when the presents are exhibited.

The friends of the bridegroom, and unacquainted with the bride, should send their presents to him, and he should send them to the house of the bride's mother after having written notes of thanks to the givers.

Christening Presents.—With regard to christening presents the godfathers and godmothers are expected to make presents to their godchild; these should be sent the day before the christening, and should consist of a silver mug and silver fork and spoon from the godfathers, while a lace robe or handsome cloak are usual presents from the godmothers. A present of money from £1 to £5 should be made to the nurse on the day of the christening when the godparents are relatives, but oftener than not the sponsors are represented by proxy.

Gratuities to Servants.—The only fee expected from ladies after paying a visit of some days, is one to the housemaid, which ranges from 5s. to 10s., according to the length of the visit. Young ladies give even less when visiting by themselves, 2s. 6d. being considered sufficient for a short visit and 5s. for a longer one.

The fees expected from gentlemen are, To the butler or footman who valets them and to the coachman if he drives them to and from the station or takes charge of their horses, and to the housemaid. The fee to the butler or footman who acts as valet is for a long visit from 10s. to £1, and for a short visit from 3s. to 5s. To the coachman from 2s. 6d. to 5s. in the first case, and from 10s. to £1 in the second. To the housemaid, 2s. 6d. to 10s. For fees to gamekeeper see page 223.

CHAPTER XLVII

Christening Parties may be said to be strictly family gatherings, only the near relatives of the parents being invited on these occasions.

The Invitations are given in friendly notes, and are not issued on "at home" cards. The notice averages from a week to ten days according to circumstances, meaning the health and strength of the infant's mother.

As a Rule Six Weeks are allowed to elapse between the birth of the child and the date of the christening.

The Relatives are either invited to luncheon after the ceremony, or to a reception tea, or to a dinner-party to be given the same evening. If a luncheon is decided upon it generally takes place at 1.30, or earlier, immediately on the return from the church. The meal usually consists of hot viands—game or poultry—not substantial joints. Hot and cold sweets. Fruit to follow. A smart christening cake should occupy the centre of the table. Champagne, claret, and sherry are given, although the former is probably the only one of the three drunk on the occasion; this, when the health of the infant is proposed—the only health which finds acceptance at these gatherings.

The Guests go in to Luncheon quite informally, the ladies and hostess entering first, followed by the men guests and the host. They should be seated at table by the help of name cards, each lady being placed at the right hand of a gentleman. The clergyman who performs the ceremony, if a friend, should sit at the hostess's left hand, and should be asked to say grace; but in town he seldom joins these family gatherings unless well acquainted with his parishioners.

A **Reception Tea,** when given, is served in the dining-room; but in this case the guests are received on arrival by the hostess in the drawing-room, and when all have arrived, she accompanies them to the tea-room and remains there with them. The maid-servants should pour out and hand the tea and coffee across the tea-table, but the hostess should hand the cakes, etc., to her relatives, assisted by the host, if present. The refreshments consist of the usual variety in confectionery seen at all smart " at homes," a christening cake being the addition.

Christening Dinner-Parties closely resemble all other family functions of this nature, with the exception that the infant's health is drunk at dessert, and that a christening cake is placed opposite the hostess when the table is cleared for dessert.

The Christening Ceremony takes place in the morning, usually at 12.30. The relatives on arrival at the church seat themselves in pews or on chairs near to the font. The godmother holds the infant during the first part of the service, and then places it on the left arm of the officiating clergyman. One of the godfathers should name the child in response to the clergyman's question. If the child is a girl, two godmothers and one godfather are necessary. If a boy, two godfathers and one godmother are required. These godparents are usually the intimate friends of the child's mother. In certain instances the

relatives are chosen for the office of godfather and godmother, but oftener not for family reasons.

Christening Presents vary according to means and
inclination, and often comprise gifts of jewellery when the
infant is a girl, and money and silver plate if a boy; silver
spoons, forks, mugs, bowls, etc. The selection is a wide
one, and nothing comes amiss, from a robe with fine lace
to a chain and pendant or a jewelled watch. These
presents are usually sent the day previous to that of the
christening.

Fees and Tips.—Only minor fees are given to those
assisting at the ceremony. The officiating priest receives
some little gift in old silver or china, but not of money;
if, however, the parents of the child are wealthy a cheque
is sometimes given with a request that he will devote it
to the needs of his parish.

Tips to the nurse from the child's godparents vary from
five shillings to a sovereign according to individual means.

INDEX

THE END

PRINTED BY
WILLIAM CLOWES AND SONS, LIMITED,
LONDON AND BECCLES.

2013037R20151

Printed in Great Britain
by Amazon.co.uk, Ltd.,
Marston Gate.